"Evelio Grillo's memoir *Black Cuban,* ... memories of my own family's movements from Cuba to Tampa, Florida . . . Grillo **brings the period to life . . . I strongly recommend this book.**"

—John Mason,
author of *Black Gods: Orisha Studies in the New World*

"**The fascinating odyssey of a remarkable life.** . . How did this visionary and appealing man become the pioneer and influential leader that he is? Reading his history, a part of which he brilliantly shares with us now, helps us grasp some of the early values, cultural forces, and relationships that formed him and influenced his choices."

—Herman Gallegos,
National Council of La Raza and
National Community Service Organization

"Evelio Grillo shares with us his rich and complex history—unique in its combination of cultures and events, yet shared in its themes of honoring our heritage, melding diverse traditions, and carving out one's own identity . . . An **insightful and inspiring** work."

—U.S. Congresswoman Barbara Lee

"Grillo's testimonial presents colorful descriptions of the interaction between the black and the white American and Cuban communities. His detailed memories of the struggle of these communities, and of their slow and shy interactions, offer an **excellent interdisciplinary approach to multiculturalism . . . Highly recommended for African and Latino studies collections and for all students and scholars researching immigration.**"

—R. Ocasio,
CHOICE

"**Grillo proudly embraces his dual heritage as both black American and black Cuban** . . . The quality of Grillo's writing, the unique local significance of his subject and the prestigious sponsorship of his publication combine to make this a very attractive book. It should be included in high school and middle school curricula, and it will appeal for a wide readership interested in the history of Tampa.

—Susan Greenbaum
The Tampa Tribune-Times

Recovering the U.S. Hispanic Literary Heritage

Board of Editorial Advisors

Black Cuban, Black American
A Memoir

Evelio Grillo

Introduction by Kenya Dworkin y Méndez

Recovering the U.S. Hispanic Literary Heritage

Arte Público Press
Houston, Texas
2000

This volume is made possible through grants from the National Endowment for the Arts (a federal agency), the Rockefeller Foundation, the Charles Stewart Mott Foundation, the Lila Wallace-Reader's Digest Fund and the City of Houston through The Cultural Arts Council of Houston, Harris County.

Recovering the past, creating the future

Arte Público Press
University of Houston
Houston, Texas 77204-2174

Cover design by Ken Bullock

Cover photograph, and all interior photographs, courtesy of the author

Grillo, Evelio.
  Black Cuban, Black American : a memoir / by Evelio Grillo.
  p.   cm.
  ISBN 1-55885-293-X (alk. paper)
  1. Grillo, Evelio. 2. Cuban Americans—Biography. I. Title.

E184.C97 G73   2000
973'.04687291—dc21   00-020774

♾ The paper used in this publication meets the requirements of the American National Standard for Information Sciences—Permanence of Paper for Printed Library Materials, ANSI Z39.48-1984.

Introduction © 2000 by Kenya Dworkin y Méndez

1 2 3 4 5 6 7 8 9   0 9 8 7 6 5 4 3 2

CONTENTS

PHOTOGRAPHS

(*photographs begin following page 78*)

[1.] *Antonio Grillo.*

[2.] *The Grillo family circa 1920.*

[3.] *Amparo Grillo in the early 1930s.*

[4.] *At Dunbar High School, Washington, D.C.*

[5.] *Xavier University, New Orleans.*

[6.] *Private Grillo, 1942.*

[7.] *The Grillo family in 1947.*

[8.] *A life of service.*

Introduction

[T]he American pattern of rigid segregation of blacks and whites asserted itself with unrestrained, brutal vigor. For all of our sharing of language, culture, and religion with white Cubans, we black Cubans were black. When the school bell rang, we joined the streams of children headed toward the "colored" schools. School resolved all of my confusion about my color, my Spanish tongue, and my culture. I was a black boy. *That's* what was important![1]

HOWEVER SELF-EVIDENT THE TRUTH of the above words might seem, when considered in context they reveal an anxiety, a racial and ethnic identity crisis, that few Hispanics or black Americans have ever brought to the fore. This because in the U. S. framework of racial and ethnic politics, Hispanics and black Americans—and whites, for that matter—seldom overlap; they are not allowed to. A glance at a present-day government form or loan application, with racial categories such as "white (non-Hispanic)," "black (non-Hispanic)," and "Hispanic," seems to confirm that neither whites nor blacks can be Hispanic, regardless of their national origin, cultural heritage, or ethnic affiliation.[2]

The attitudes that brought about the institutionalization of these ill-conceived categories are not new. In the specific context of white and black Hispanics, they are the result of a century-old clash between two different notions of race and ethnicity—one Latin American, in which national identity and culture supercede race, the other U. S. American, in which race supercedes other factors.

---

[1] Excerpt from first paragraph of Chapter 7 of *Black Cuban, Black American.*

[2] It is noteworthy that in the United States Census 2000 there are three categories for gathering racial and ethnic information instead of one—ethnic self-identification, "Spanish/Hispanic/ Latino" (with space for specific information); racial self-identification (which permits one to account from multiple categories); and ancestry/heredity (for one's national or ancestral origin, or that of one's forbears).

Evelio Grillo, the octogenarian author of *Black Cuban, Black American,* grew up caught between the dramatically different worlds of *cubanidad* and African-Americanness as young black Cuban boy in Tampa.[3] As the epigraph to this essay suggests, he and many other black Cubans in the United States faced a forced walk down a particular path to school—and through life—not so much because of ethnic, racial, or class differences as on account of legally and socially sanctioned convention in the Jim Crow South. Ironically, what began as an institutionalized narrowing of choices for Grillo brought his social and political liberation, through his assimilation into the black American community. *Black Cuban, Black American* is the story of one Afro-Cuban's adventures in identity reconstruction. It is Evelio Grillo's intimate account of his costly but effective triumph over racial and ethnic ambiguity and disempowerment—a journey from Afro-Cubanness to African-Americanness. This is a journey many have made, but few, if any, have heretofore written about. Grillo's sophisticated memoir sheds light on seldom-discussed issues of Hispanicity with relation to blackness and the black experience in the United States. Though he is just one of many to have navigated the difficult waters of segregation, civil-rights activism, and the maelstrom of minority politics, the particular details of his life in a *barrio* and his escape to mainstream black American society are undeniably unique. They are not at all representative of the black Cuban experience in Ybor City—if such a generalization can indeed be made.[4]

Cubans (white or black) and other immigrants (mostly Spaniards and Sicilians) were no strangers to the rapidly growing city of Tampa, Florida, in the 1920s and 1930s. Much of the city's economic expansion was directly attributable to "Latin" immigrants, who in 1886 brought with them the cigar-making industry.[5] This revolutionized the local economy and turned Tampa into the "clear Havana" cigar capital of the world, a dynamic new city in the New South.[6] Black and white Cubans by the thousands were employed in that industry for several generations and, by the 1930s, Latins represented twenty-five percent of the city's total population, giving Tampa a distinctly

[3]*Cubanidad,* or Cubanness, a sense of Cuban identity.
[4]For an overview of the black Cuban experience in Ybor City, see Susan D. Greenbaum, *Afro-Cubans in Ybor City. A Centennial History* (Tampa: University of South Florida, 1986).
[5]"Latin," an in-group and out-group term referring to Cuban, Spanish, and Italian immigrants to Tampa. Eventually used to refer to the group collectively, e.g., Tampa Latins.
[6]For a general account of the founding of Ybor City and its social and industrial development, see Gary R. Mormino and George E. Pozetta, *The Immigrant World of Ybor City: Italians and Their Latin Neighbors* (University of Chicago, 1987).

cosmopolitan flavor. With their distinct culture and politics, Cubans made an indelible mark on what would eventually evolve into *tampeño* culture, a way of life that survives even today, over a century after the first Cubans came to Tampa from Key West and Cuba.[7]

Yet, despite the city's multicultural population, Tampa was deeply divided along Jim Crow lines. The majority of the Latin population, most of which was working-class, lived in restricted areas, ethnic enclaves in the vicinity of Tampa's hundreds of cigar factories. While there was relative tolerance towards black Cubans in the Latin quarter (where most neighborhoods and cigar factories were integrated), Ybor City and its counterpart, West Tampa, were areas that bordered on other restricted sections—areas for U. S. blacks *or* whites only. Racial discrimination was much more subtle and less deleterious within the Latin quarter than without, but it was there, nonetheless.

In the Jim-Crow South, being Cuban—even white Cuban—brought with it several limitations. White Cubans in Tampa did not fit the U. S. stereotype of the typical European immigrant as did Spaniards and Sicilians. Yes, the white Cubans had European antecedents, but they also came from an island society in which whites and blacks had coexisted for nearly five hundred years, a place where blood and culture had irremediably mixed. The perceived purity of white Cubans' racial and cultural origins was doubted even by their immigrant neighbors. They were also widely viewed as the most politically troublesome and least upwardly mobile immigrant group in Tampa because of their staunch unionism, transience, and low incidence of home ownership when compared to Spaniards and Sicilians. This perception was even more strongly held concerning black Cubans, who were often the first to be let go during lulls in Tampa's cigar-making business. Factors responsible for the higher degree of transience among Cubans included

- the legally unrestricted nature of travel to and from Cuba for much of the early twentieth century;
- the geographical proximity of Cuba to Tampa, which made such travel comparatively easy and inexpensive;
- the tradition of following cigar-factory jobs from Tampa to Havana and vice versa whenever slowdowns or strikes affected either place;
- the relatively lower salaries earned by Cubans, who rarely rose to managerial positions in the cigar industry.

---

[7]*Tampeño* is a Spanish word that functions as either an adjective, e.g., *tampeño* culture (Tampa Latin culture), or a noun, e.g., a *tampeño* (a Tampa Latin person).

These socio-ethnic and class-related factors were enough to make acceptance into mainstream society difficult—not impossible, but extremely difficult indeed. In Tampa, epithets such as *Cuban nigger* (which referred to white Cubans) and *tally wop* (which referred to black Cubans) were added to other, already existing expressions of racial and ethnic intolerance. Even popular swimming spots such as Clearwater Beach posted warnings about restrictions—NO CUBANS OR DOGS ALLOWED being one variant until the early 1960s.[8] In such a society, only deculturation and assimilation could eventually clear the path for upward mobility among Cubans after several generations. This required, among other things, a denial of African heritage and a celebration of Iberian culture, which brought white Cubans closer to their Spanish brethren and left black Cubans in the lurch. One of Latin Tampa's most enduring images of itself—one that for decades served to attract tourism to both the Latin quarter and the city at large—was one of castanet-clicking, flamenco-dancing Spanish *señoritas* in dramatic locations all over Ybor City, with an occasional white-skinned, rhumba-dancing couple thrown in for effect. Blackness, and Cubanness, for that matter, were blanched out of much of the local imagery, leaving a sepia-toned image into which many scholars and activists alike are only now trying to re-infuse color both real and symbolic.

So, if being white and ethnic was a considerable obstacle to entering mainstream society, it is not hard to imagine the difficulty encountered by immigrants both Cuban and black. Whereas lines were clearly drawn for Tampa's black Americans, immigrant blacks—who spoke Spanish, had Hispanic culture, and were set off by a higher literacy rate and better earning power than their black American counterparts—thoroughly challenged the established notions of race.[9] They unwittingly disrupted the social order. Thus, black Cubans were doubly (but not equally) marginalized by members of their own communities and outsiders. They faced an often confusing but always brutal version of Jim Crow, the confusion stemming as much from the superficial racial tolerance of their white Latin neighbors as from the larger

[8]"Tally Wop" is derived thus: Italian > *tally* and "without papers" > *wop*.
[9]The cigar makers who came from Cuba were urban folks from Havana, the island's capital city, where they received schooling and were accustomed to city ways, e.g., theaters and social clubs. These factors, combined with the fact that cigar makers earned more than most working-class laborers, often put black Cubans in better socio-economic position than their black American counterparts.

society's difficulty in classifying them. Being black, as Grillo eventually realized, was the *only* thing that really mattered in Tampa.

As a black Cuban living on the border between Latin and black American ghettos, Evelio Grillo felt very much less at home with his white Cuban
counterparts in Ybor City than he did with his black American schoolmates at
an all-black parochial school. This was truly a travesty, since, as Grillo points
out, there was a great deal black Cubans held in common with the lighter-
skinned Cubans of Ybor City—including language, culture, religion, and
history. The predominantly white Cuban community had not so long ago
shared José Martí's dream of a society in which "[a] true man [was] more than
simply a 'white,' 'black,' or 'mulatto,'" but they soon abandoned that aspira-
tion.[10] Segregation tore asunder any semblance of Cuban unity almost before
the blood spilled by Martí, Antonio Maceo, and countless others during the
war for independence from Spain had dried.[11] Motivated by either Jim Crow-
style segregation, traditional Cuban racism, or both, the white Cubans of Ybor
City saw their only strategy for acceptance into Tampa society as separation
from their black Cuban neighbors. Tampa's once-united white and black
Cubans went their different ways: the whites towards assimilation and upward
mobility, the blacks down an apparent dead-end street.

White Cubans created the Círculo Cubano, a comprehensive mutual-aid
society that stands even today, with the help of grant money and membership
drives that have targeted many middle- to upper-class Cubans and non-
Cubans alike. This organization now boasts a recently formed "Mambi Club,"
named for the mostly black Cubans who fought for Cuba in the 1895 war for
independence. It is a noble name for a club whose membership is almost
exclusively white and professional. On the other hand, Black Cubans, who are
the true descendants of most of the *mambis* and who never instituted racial
restrictions on membership, left the Círculo Cubano and established the
Unión Martí-Maceo. This multi-story edifice, also a mutual-aid society, was
the only Latin mutual-aid building to crumble under the wrecking-ball of federal "urban renewal" in the early 1960s. Its membership had dwindled
severely, due to Depression-era and later transience caused by unemployment,

[10]José Martí, considered by many to be the father of Cuban independence, visited Tampa twenty
times in four years. There he found staunch spiritual and financial support among the city's
black and white Cuban cigar makers, as well as others. The quote, a translation, is from John
M. Kirk's *José Martí: Mentor of the Cuban Nation* (Gainesville: University Presses of Florida,
1983), 112.
[11]Antonio Maceo, a leading general in the Cuban War of Independence (1895-1898) and a mulatto, was as much an icon of the Cuban struggle for independence as was José Martí.

which always affected blacks more severely than whites. However, the remaining members (combined with new members and those who left but later returned) managed to secure and keep a small, inelegant building in Ybor City, staving off the Unión Martí-Maceo's total disappearance. They have valiantly struggled for survival and are even now actively engaged in rescue and revival. Both clubs engaged in centennial celebrations in 1999-2000 as each approached the hundredth anniversary of their respective clubs (and their membership's separation) in significantly different ways. There is discussion of "reconciliation"—more from the Martí-Maceo side than from the Círculo's—in the form of collaborative educational and social programs, but a huge disparity exists in the monies available to each. One reason is that the white Cubans' club building is eligible for historic-preservation funds, while the black Cubans' is not. Thus the white club has both money and an elegant edifice; the black club has neither. Even the discrepant financial situation, however, is not nearly as tragic as the historic reasons for the separation of the two clubs. The celebrations also mark the year when former footsoldiers for racial equality abandoned a goal that even today, a hundred years later, seems painfully out of reach, whether in the United States or in Cuba. The mood of these two clubs' birthday celebrations should be bittersweet at the very least, but time has a way of dimming memory and dulling pain.

That Evelio Grillo was offered an alternative to what seemed to be his ordained destiny—and this by people even more marginalized and discriminated against than he—is what makes this story so very extraordinary. Through equal measures of good fortune and hard work, Grillo was able to elude ethnic and racial isolation in Tampa and enter the world of black America, a place with a long tradition of struggle and self-realization, with recognized heroes and heroines. For all the heroism of so many black Cubans, Grillo had never learned much about them, not from his fellow Cubans nor from the nuns who taught him at the all-black St. Peter Claver school. As Grillo put it, "They couldn't teach me how to *be* black."[12] The struggle for his heart and mind was won by the likes of Frederick Douglass, Nat Turner, and Sojourner Truth. His journey—from Tampa to Washington, New Orleans, and beyond—was a liberating and empowering experience, one that would not have been possible had he not been taught to feel "unambiguously black." Even in India, where he served during World War II, Grillo found a way to transform racially oppressive circumstances into the unprecedented establishment of integrated sporting events and social activities, as well as the

[12]Interview with Evelio Grillo, August, 1999.

publication of a daily newsletter that rivaled the official military newspaper. In general, Evelio Grillo's detailed description of the lives of black service-men in a segregated army sheds much light on yet another chapter of U. S. race-relations history that has long begged attention.

Black Cuban, Black American is, in a sense, two books. The first half reads like a classic coming-of-age story, the second like a wartime diary. In fact, one is left with a strong sense that there is another part yet to come, thus documenting the *entire* life of an extraordinary man. While in school, partic-ularly after going to Washington, D.C., Evelio Grillo fulfilled the dream of a small group of middle-class Tampa blacks by "going up there [north] and showing them what a southern colored boy could do." In the process, he com-pleted his metamorphosis from confused Cuban boy into confidant black American man. That Grillo was given access to an elite education, especially a university degree, distinguishes him from so many of his Tampa counter-parts, a fact he addresses quite openly in his candid memoir. While Grillo was finishing his education in Washington, D.C., and New Orleans, most black Cubans in Tampa were migrating north to industrial cities such as New York, Chicago and Philadelphia to continue a strictly working-class existence. In cities like New York, where they joined communities of other Hispanics, some former *tampeños* did finally make it into the middle-class and beyond through hard work and, sometimes, higher education. Grillo, on the other hand, went from a special high school in Washington, D. C., to earn a bachelor's degree in New Orleans and, later, a master's degree in California.

In the army, Grillo proved his mettle for political and social organizing, talents that would serve him richly after the war. He was able to synthesize the entirety of his experience and put it to work for working-class people, partic-ularly blacks and Mexican Americans, over the ensuing decades. This is the portion of his story that he shares with us only briefly in the epilogue—a part of his life that he is not yet entirely comfortable talking about. Ironically, despite the fact he had left his Cubanness so far behind—so much so that it seemed to have been "educated out" of him—it was precisely this alter ego that permitted his success as an organizer among Spanish-speaking people. The *persona* left back in Tampa reemerged in Oakland decades later to help him earn the trust and respect of Mexican-American workers. Without his *cubano* self this would not have been easy; even then, when he was a crucial link between the Mexican-American community and the greater political scene, he found himself again facing a lesson learned long ago—that he was "too black to be Hispanic." Having once been forced to make a choice between Cuban and African American, he could still, some forty years after his birth, be only one or the other. Racial and ethnic divisions, as well as stark class differences, still prevailed. Sadly, only by subordinating his Cuban identity was Evelio Grillo able to buy a one-ticket out of the *barrio* and into the black mainstream. Fortunately for him—and for us—he never entirely gave up his Cuban identity. As a member of the black mainstream, with surviving vestiges of his Cuban self, he offers us a book filled with eighty years worth of lessons. This book forces us to question, perceiving with an insight beyond our years, the racial and ethnic categories that continue to operate in contemporary American society.

Kenya Dworkin y Méndez
Carnegie Mellon University

Acknowledgments

IT IS EXHILARATING to be able to recognize the prime nurturers in my life, for nurture turns out to be the greatest gift we receive from others once the importance of genetics is admitted. Therefore the writing of acknowledgements presents me with a challenge of some magnitude, for my mentors were legion.

All of these played large roles in my development: Mr. Nicholas Hezekiah Martin, role model's epitome; Dr. Howard Thurman, who became my father; Mrs. Sue Bailey Thurman, who constantly sought mind-opening opportunities for me; Sister Mary Felicity, an utterly dedicated principal who gave her life to the education of black children; Sister Mary Elise, love incarnate and developer of my soul; Dr. Eliot Studt, who patiently developed the professional in me; and Mrs. Albina Blanchett, in whose lap I learned to read.

Yet, as measured by the days and hours dedicated to my care and development, my mother—like all mothers—stands alone. My sister, Sylvia, joins her in that unparalleled place reserved for them. However difficult they were to love, they mothered me.

In this season, the heading-in period of my life, I believe that all those with whom I have been close—and legions whom I have never seen nor heard—have played major roles in my growth and development. But I realize, with the only maturity I shall ever know, that my mother was chief among the villagers who reared me, however modest was her goal: keeping me out of jail!

At the age of fifteen, I had to steel myself for what I knew would be a major confrontation. Mr. Martin had announced that he would take me to some clearly fabulous land called Up North to "get an education." On that occasion, I felt a power I had never known before. And her face was drawn with a sadness I had never seen before.

"Are you sure you want to do this?" she asked me, in despair.

"Mama," I said, firmly and without hesitation, "there is not very much for me in Tampa. I did not do well in school this past year. I am afraid that if I stay here, I may do worse."

She turned away and began to gather my clothes. It was her way of indicating resignation to the inevitable.

Mr. Martin had posed the difficult challenge of asking that I bring five dollars with me for the trip. She solved that problem by pawning her wedding ring for that amount—to redeem it in two weeks for seven dollars and fifty cents.

Although she was usually too tired, and too beset, to baby me, and although she had little capacity for hugging and cuddling, she gave me all that she had to give me—every bit. That was a great deal indeed, as I have come to realize: the most that any person has contributed to me, to my growth, to my development as a member of the human family. I feared her. I resented her. I sought in vain for her approbation. I took her every word as a command to be a "good boy." As I have attempted to develop loving, intimate relationships with women, I have become aware of the pervasiveness, and the endurance, of her influence. Yet I know that, above the legions of my mentors and role models, she stands alone as the lighter of my paths through life's labyrinths.

And so this memoir is dedicated to her, and to my sister, who—between the screaming fights—carried the primary, day-by-day responsibilities for my physical care.

Evelio Grillo
May, 2000

To
AMPARO VALDÉS GRILLO
and to
SYLVIA GRILLO GRIÑÁN

PART ONE

Ybor City

CHAPTER 1

Father

IT HAD TO BE A SATURDAY AFTERNOON because of the way the house smelled, the way that it felt, and the way that it sounded. I had been home all day, rather than at Mrs. Byna's, the neighbor who took care of me during the week while my mother worked.

Saturday afternoon was special. Mother would be home from work early, the house would be immaculately clean, and the wonderful smells of a more than ordinary meal would fill the air.

Perhaps we would have *biftec a la palomilla*—thin slices of sirloin seared rapidly in olive oil and smothered with onions—rice, cold boiled string beans, and a simply magnificent salad of lettuce, vine-ripened tomatoes from our own garden, and large avocado slices.

Framed in the doorway between the kitchen and the back porch, Mother and Father spoke intensely to each other. From the floor of the back porch, where I was playing with a new toy, I heard him ask in disbelief: "Haven't you packed his clothes yet?"

"I didn't know he was going," she replied, her face filled with apprehension.

Quickly and sternly he came back: "Either Chuchi goes or I won't go."

I remember vividly my mother's sad, resigned face as she turned from my father and walked dejectedly back into the kitchen, all hope of keeping me with her now gone.

The puzzle came together years later: "Chuchi" was my father's nickname for me. He was going to Cuba, to attempt to recover from tuberculosis, which he had contracted, and I was to accompany him.

Only the vaguest impressions of my father exist in my mind. My mother kept absolutely silent about him. She must have been very angry with him, for I do not remember her mentioning his name to us children, not even once.

3

Scratching around for information, I have learned that he had been drinking quite heavily and that he gambled. While reluctant to soil his memory, an aunt has hinted obliquely that he was a womanizer.

My earliest memory of myself involved my father, whose vague form I can recall, barely. But I have very vivid memories of his presence. I would sit on the front porch, waiting for him to come home from work. When the trolley car came past our house, I would run excitedly to the corner to greet him as he got off, at the end of the block. That's all, a vignette that plays in my mind over and over.

The very next morning my father and I took the ship for Cuba, the S. S. *Havana*. That ship and its sister vessel, the S. S. *Cuba,* handled the lively trade between Havana and Tampa. I believe my father carried me in his arms up the gangplank. Then he put me down, took my hand, and walked me to our room on board.

I felt very special, my hand in his, looking across the infinite distance between his shoulder and my face. It was the last time our father saw his family, except for me. I remember little of the trip over, only the departure, and that only vaguely.

We went to live at the home of one of my father's sisters. Again, without remembering his face, I remember walks with him, especially one walk, when we returned with a bag of large grapefruit that he had bought for me.

My memory jumps to a very dramatic scene. Sitting in a rocking chair, father hemorrhaged torrents of blood from his mouth into a large white enamelware bucket. My aunts and uncles tended to him with cloths and with expressions of love and concern. One aunt stayed with me, keeping me a distance from the tragedy, but letting me see the entire development, although I did not see my father die.

My next memory is of the wake and the funeral. The mourners came in little horse-and-buggy rigs, to attend what I later concluded was the wake. The first casket was refrigerated. Water slowly dripped into a bucket placed under it, to catch the melting ice. I never looked into the casket, or, if I did, I don't recall the experience. The mechanics of the melting ice and of the water dripping into the bucket under the coffin absorbed all of my fascinated attention.

In the morning, some men came and took the refrigerated coffin out of the house. They must have switched the remains to the coffin in which my father was to be buried. They brought that more elegant coffin into the house, placing it exactly where the refrigerated coffin had been. I recall a lot of people dressed in black milling about the house.

The aunt who was taking care of me carried me out to the balcony, and held her arms around me as the funeral cortege formed. A sea of horses and buggies, and one very ornate vehicle, the hearse, crowded the street. Then, slowly, the cortege moved out. I watched, fascinated. I had no idea that I was saying goodbye to my father.

I recall little that followed until some time later, when I was on a ship on my way back to Tampa and my mother. A friend of the family named Nicolás took me back. I remember looking at the sea through the railings, and the magnificent hat that my aunts must have bought for me. It was broad-brimmed, a pretty ribbon cascading down its side, just the thing to draw admiring comments from older people giving attention to a very vain little boy.

How and when we landed are all lost memories, for I was not yet four.

CHAPTER 2

Black Cubans and White Cubans

WHILE MAINTAINING ITS IDENTITY as a distinctly Latin community, Ybor City, my birthplace, lies completely within the city of Tampa, Florida, which governs it. Culturally, socially, and economically a small city within a city, its residents were a mixture of white Cubans, Italians, black Cubans, black Americans, Spaniards, and a not very visible number of white Americans of European extraction.

During the years between roughly 1880 and 1930, Tampa flourished at the center of the worldwide cigar-making industry. A great portion of the industry was in Ybor City, giving Tampa the identity of "Cigar-Making Capital of the World."

Ybor City (pronounced *EE-bor*) took its name from Vicente Martínez Ybor, one of the earliest manufacturers to build a cigar factory in Tampa.

My parents were part of the large migration of Cubans who settled in Ybor City seeking jobs in the fledgling industry. My father, Antonio, worked as a "finisher," a very prestigious job involving the final sculpture of the cigars into identical shapes. My mother, Amparo, worked as a *bonchera*, a "buncher." She gathered the inner leaves of the cigars into the long, rounded shapes to which the finishers applied the final, prime, wrapping leaf.

While the preferred tobacco for cigars still grew in Cuba, the making of a very large proportion of the finished product, the actual cigars, took place in the United States. This strategy yielded enormous economic benefits. The machinery and materials needed to make and package the cigars abounded in the United States. Tariffs on the finished product presented no costs if it was manufactured in the United States.

Moreover, the United States provided the primary market for cigars. Enough trade moved back and forth between Tampa and Havana to support two round trips a week by the shipping line which served the ports.

6

Black Cubans and white Cubans migrated by the thousands from Cuba. Legal separation of the two races did not prevail in Cuba as it did in United States, but discrimination along racial lines and separation along social and economic lines did exist. In Cuba, affluent black Cubans moved within the society of the affluent. *"Es Negro, pero es Negro blanco"* (He is a black man, but he is a white black man) was an expression I heard often.

Separation of the races by residence was not practiced, although separation by economic class made for *de facto* segregation by race, since discrimination kept black Cubans in a second-class position, economically. Blacks generally did not live in luxurious houses.

However, commercial and governmental facilities were accessible to all in Cuba. Blacks attended, taught, and served as administrators in the schools. Blacks used the hospitals and clinics without limitation, and served as staff members in most capacities. Blacks also served in the military without restrictions. The general who had led the Cuban revolution against Spain was a dark mulatto, Antonio Maceo. As Cubans entered Ybor City, however, they were sorted out. Black Cubans went to a neighborhood, immediately east of Nebraska Avenue, inhabited by black Americans and a scattering of poor whites. White Cubans had a much wider range of choices, though most of them chose to remain in Ybor City. A scattering went to live in West Tampa, across the river, in a sparsely developed section of the larger city.

Nebraska Avenue formed the western boundary of Ybor City. Twenty-second Street formed, roughly, the eastern boundary. The avenues ran east and west, with Sixteeneth Avenue forming a northern limit, and Sixth Avenue a southern one. From Sixteenth Avenue to roughly Twenty-second Avenue were scattered more affluent white Cubans and Italians and Spaniards, some living a semi-rural life, with a cow or two, goats, and chickens.

Black Cubans worked in the factories alongside white Cubans. While my mother formed interracial friendships at work, few, if any, such friendships extended to visits in the homes. Nor did whites and blacks attend church together. Black Cubans had their own mutual benefit society and social center, La Union Martí-Maceo.

Black Cubans and white Cubans worked side by side in the cigar-making industry. But I know of only one black Cuban who won a status above that of worker: Facundo Accion, who achieved the highly honored position of *lector,* the reader.

Black Cubans and white Cubans interacted in the streets and in public places such as grocery stores, produce stands, meat markets, and in the corner saloon, where men who were not at work gathered in the afternoon to watch the throwing of the *bolita* bag, and the selection of the day's number, which paid lucky ticket holders five dollars for every penny waged.

Bolita was Tampa's version of the numbers game. A hundred small balls, each numbered, were placed in a cloth bag. A small crowd of men gathered to watch the proceedings. At the appointed hour, the bag, carefully sewn tight under the watchful eyes of the onlookers, was thrown randomly across the room to an onlooker. He, in turn, would gather one ball carefully into his hand, through the cloth of the bag, and let the other ninety-nine dangle below. One person tied a string around the lucky numbered ball and cut that section of the cloth away.

Finally, the person holding the lucky ball showed it and announced the number. Within minutes, the word rushed throughout the town, so the lucky ones could celebrate their good fortune and the unlucky ones could bemoan their fate. That is why the populace described the process as "throwing the number." That this racket enjoyed "protection" from the authorities appeared obvious. No attempt was made to hide the ceremony, held daily at the same time and in the same place.

Blacks and whites visited back and forth at wakes and funerals. A white Cuban or two might show up at the spiritualist seances to which my mother dragged me weekly. Blacks and whites belonged to the same grocery cooperative and to the same pre-pay health clinic.

My mother also took me to one meeting of a labor union, which held its meetings and celebrations in a modern labor temple. As a child, I attended a meeting held in connection with a strike or the threat of one.

Then there was baseball, to which the entire town paid homage, under the leadership of Al Lopez, legendary catcher of the Brooklyn Dodgers and a native of Ybor City. He spent much of his winters in Tampa basking in the glory of his fame.

During the World Series the local Spanish-language daily newspaper provided an elaborate mechanical display which represented the action from wherever the games were being played. Shiny metal balls represented the players, and the game could be followed as the balls moved around a magnetic board representing the playing field.

It seemed that the entirety of Ybor City gathered in front of the mesmerizing display, cheering or booing depending upon the course of the game. This was one activity I could enjoy without special permission from Mother. Many elder male friends of the family would keep watchful eyes on me. That kept her from worrying.

That was the extent of the limited association between black Cubans and white Cubans. I don't remember playing with a single white Cuban child. I remember the faces of only three white Cuban men who came to the house, two as music teachers and one as a stout, jolly Sunday boarder whom we called "*Tío* Pío."

With the exception of the local corner bar, which they could patronize, black Cubans did not share recreational activities with white Cubans. They were not hired as clerks, or even as menial help in the restaurants. There were no black Cuban entrepreneurs except for a tailor, a barber, and a very successful dry-cleaning establishment.

In the main, black Cubans and white Cubans lived apart from one another in Ybor City.

CHAPTER 3

Black Cubans and
Black Americans

IN THE GHETTO WITHIN A GHETTO located in the southwest corner of Ybor City, formed by Nebraska and Sixth Avenues, black Cubans and black Americans lived together. Black Cubans formed the larger group in this neighborhood. Neither group held local political power. A very few men developed limited power by extracting favors from the ruling groups of white Americans, and, later, of Italian Americans.

Most black Americans lived west of Nebraska Avenue. No black Cubans lived there. This large section of the city above Nebraska housed solidly black American neighborhoods. They could be distinguished along social and economic lines. The closer to Ybor City, the poorer they were. The farther west one walked, towards the main shopping and commercial streets of Tampa, the more substantial the homes became and the more elaborate became the landscaping.

Public elementary schools functioned in this section, as did large black churches and funeral parlors. The Central Life Insurance Company, an important enterprise in the black American community, had its operations there also.

Central Avenue provided the bustling commercial center. Along its seven- or eight-block stretch were found the offices of the local dentist and the local doctor; a large drugstore (complete with modern fountain); the storefront "colored" branch of the public library; a shoemaker; two barber shops; several restaurants; real estate offices; the town's largest saloon, Moon's; the "colored" movie house, the Central Theater; and various other small businesses.

No single broad statement can encompass the relationship between black Cubans and their American counterparts. At the time of my birth, my mother's family had lived in the United States twenty-five or more years. Mother had attended elementary school in Jacksonville, Florida. This still made us rank newcomers, for black Americans traced their ancestry back for more than three centuries in the United States.

10

Our parents all came from Cuba and spoke little or no English. Differences in language and culture became formidable impediments to full integration of black Cubans within the black American community.

While black Cuban children became fluent in English, our parents could not navigate the difficult waters of language and culture. Within our homes and in the Cuban community, we spoke Spanish. These factors lent an edgy quality to the interactions between black Cubans and black Americans. This touchiness arose as a natural consequence of the vastly different experiences which the slave ancestors of Cuban blacks had, as compared to the slave experiences of the ancestors of American blacks.

In Spanish-speaking countries, slaves, though subjugated and exploited, were, I believe, taught to read, write, and do arithmetic. The Spanish colonizers generally did not bring their women with them. They came seeking their fortunes, hoping to return in honor to Spain. The colonizers of the United States on the other hand, brought their women with them.

The Spanish took the only women available to them, slaves, as their concubines, and in a large number of cases, as their wives. They lived openly with their black mates. One of the vestiges of this is the custom, at least among Cuban men, of calling the woman with whom they are intimate *mi negrita,* "my little black one," be she black or white. It is a term of endearment which is considered a special part of love-making.

Laws or custom forbade the teaching of reading and writing to U.S. slaves. Establishing families was a limited option, for slaves could be sold or traded at the whim of the master or mistress. (There were exceptions. Many U. S. slaveholders treated slave children well and left them money.)

One consequence of this difference in the treatment of slaves showed itself as generations succeeded generations. In Tampa there dwelt together a highly literate population of black Cubans and a black American population in which illiteracy rates were high. The differences in language, religion, culture, and social factors lent an edgy quality to the interactions between the groups.

A common racial identity as blacks did not bridge the gulf that existed between the two groups. Black Americans spoke English and followed Protestant religions. Black Cubans spoke Spanish and practiced Catholicism.

But other realities—such as play, school, work, friendships, love, sex, and marriage—bonded young black Cubans to black Americans. It was from black Americans that we learned about black colleges, for example. We learned that we could attend them. I don't know any black Cuban college graduate of my generation, and of all the generations preceding desegregation, who is not a graduate of a historically black college.

The relatively small number of black Cubans who entered college achieved nearly full integration, socially, into black American life: the language the same, their accents the same, their dress the same. Their dating involved almost exclusively eligible black American counterparts.

Those who did not attend college went to live circumscribed lives in the Latin ghettoes of New York City, to which my generation largely migrated along with their parents. Contact with American blacks was minimal in the early days of the migration to New York City.

During the Great Depression of the early thirties they traveled to New York City in large numbers packed ten into an eight-passenger limousine, at five dollars per person, I was told. This exodus led to a vastly intensified movement of the young black Cubans, who remained in Tampa, towards black Americans. Those who stayed in Tampa enjoyed larger and larger places in black American life, as teachers, as social workers, and some as leaders in the black American community. They chose black American spouses almost exclusively. Many of them attended college, the largest number at Florida A & M, the public university for blacks.

Our choices became clear: to swim in black American society or drown in the Latin ghettoes of New York City, never to be an integral part of American life.

This is why the experience of black Cubans who joined with black Americans is so different from that of black Cubans who remained loosely tethered to the white Cuban society. Integration presented us with simple options: join the black American society, with its rich roots deep in this country, or have no American roots at all.

We had no problems with those we knew as neighbors or schoolmates, mostly teasing and name-calling. We developed close friendships flowing from our school relationships. We did not, however, visit one another's homes very often.

The age of the automobile had just begun to flower. I know of only two black Cuban families who owned automobiles. We traveled by trolley or we walked. That meant that we had to walk through the black American neighborhoods above Nebraska Avenue if we wanted to go to the Central Theater. That sometimes became a cause for fear. The black Americans who lived in the blocks immediately above Nebraska Avenue did not always accept us, particularly those of us whom they did not know because we did not attend the public schools.

The feelings were reciprocated. Our parents' fears of black Americans were transmitted to us in the home, where they lived in isolation both from the white Cuban and black American worlds.

So we young people traveled in groups, walking those dreaded blocks from Nebraska Avenue to Central Avenue and back to attend the "colored" theater to see movie heroes of the day—Tom Mix, Rin Tin Tin—and the thrilling serials.

Some of our fears had a basis in reality, though nothing as serious as we envisioned. I remember being run home from Central Avenue during one summer when I had the duty of taking a warm lunch to my sister, Sylvia, who worked as a receptionist and assistant for the local black American dentist, Dr. Ervin.

I rode the trolley to take lunch to her, thereby assuring that the food would be warm. On the way back home, however, I walked so as to save the five cents in trolley fare.

As I walked the five and one-half blocks from the trolley stop to the dentist's office, I was approached by Jason, a tall, lanky, black American classmate—a good-looking, confident boy. He had a mildly menacing look on his face. I thought I knew what he was after when he asked, "What are you doing in this part of town, Grillo?"

I had had no previous direct conversation with Jason.

"Taking lunch to my sister."

"She works around here?"

"Yes, for Dr. Ervin, down the street."

"How long are you going be up there?"

"About an hour, perhaps."

"Well, we'll be waiting for you when you come out, okay?"

"Okay!" I was intimidated, for I knew that we had no friendly business to transact with me. My tormentors, I assumed, intended to lie in wait for me, to beat me up and to do other horrible things to me. I now believe that their intent was more to scare than to harm, for I was never touched during my two years at Booker T. Washington High.

They could have had it in for me, for I had captured the attention of Pauline, an absolutely ravishing black American beauty, whom they thought belonged to them. I had had the temerity to meet Pauline at the movies twice and to walk her home the long way, where dark streets and trees provided wonderful settings for kissing and light petting.

So the fear was real and I took no chances. I came downstairs from the dentist's office and waited in the entry way of the building until certain that none of the feared group remained within a block of the building.

Dashing to an alley across the street, in the middle of the block, I lost myself quickly within it. Then, I threaded my way carefully from alley to alley, until I reached safety on the other side of Nebraska Avenue, in my own neighborhood.

This was the simple life of caste and class as it is lived out in all generations and in all places. Black Cuban cigar makers were an elite. They were highly skilled and they worked in a very intellectual environment. In Cuba, they lived in the cities, and they participated in the intellectual and political life of the nation. Their rural brothers and sisters worked in the cane and tobacco fields. They did not enjoy the same level of education and social sophistication.

Some among the Black Cuban cigar makers became poets, writers, artists, and musicians. They moved comfortably in the society of small tradesmen. They found their place, marginally between the upper-lower and lower-middle classes.

In Tampa they had substantial roles in the politics of Cuba; they helped to finance the Cuban war of independence against Spain and harbored the leaders of the insurrection. Moreover, they had a Spanish daily newspaper to read.

Between Nebraska and Central Avenues, on other hand, lived many unskilled and illiterate black Americans, living what black Cuban adults considered a rough life. Though a large number of them were middle-class in income, outlook, and way of life, very large numbers of them were clearly in the lowest economic and social classes. Interactions between our two groups increased only slowly, though steadily, until today the two are comfortably integrated as part of a larger black group.

In earlier days, however, a definite guardedness characterized the relationship between those who were not yet good friends. Our parents, who had limited contact with black Americans, sometimes spoke disparagingly of them, criticizing their behavior and attributing the violence that occurred within the lowest economic class to the entire black community.

As children, we had intensive interaction with black Americans in school. We became good friends. We studied with them, we played with them, we fell in love with them and, as we grew older, we married them. Our feelings toward them were very positive and we were sensitive to remarks critical of them.

Reciprocally, they considered us part of the black community, for that was the way we were perceived by the larger American society. Our fears of being attacked, while real, were not borne out by what actually happened. Not once were we molested. I remember only one altercation between a group of black Americans and one of black Cuban adolescents. It took place near the border between the two ghettoes. In a half-hearted rock-throwing fight that did not last very long, no one was injured, not even slightly.

We had a full calendar of community events at La Union Martí-Maceo, our own black Cuban community center: Frequent Latin dances, travelling vaudeville shows from Cuba, and an occasional play in Spanish that we staged ourselves rounded out a busy schedule for our community.

Some of the young adult black Cubans, mostly males, attended dances held by black American organizations at our center where a large dance hall was a favored venue. In the early 1930s a "colored" movie theater, constructed in Ybor City, drew nightly a thoroughly mixed crowd of black Americans and black Cubans. The theater served also as a stopping place for road shows. Our community fluttered for days in anticipation of the appearance of Cab Calloway, then at the height of his career. Generally, however, we did not attend plays, concerts, recitals, and lectures, presented in English. These were held in the large Protestant churches in the black American ghetto, where we seldom ventured, other than to attend school.

There was one week during the year, however, during which the entire black American and black Cuban communities became one. Gasparilla Day and the South Florida Fair, held in conjunction with each other and during the same week, helped greatly to cement our identities as part of one large black community.

Both communities took to the streets as one large mass, walking towards downtown Tampa to view the elaborate and exciting Gasparilla parade. Gasparilla was a pirate who, history or legend held, had roamed the waters outside of Tampa during the eighteenth century.

Tampa businessmen, dressed as pirates, rode gaily decorated floats in a long, colorful parade. We lined up for blocks to see the thrilling spectacle and to scramble for the trinkets that these pirates scattered along the route. The tradition continues to this day, and is now integrated. We have our own black pirates, now!

The South Florida Fair held two Children's Days. On the first, called simply Children's Day, all white children entered free of charge. They included some very light mulatto (mixed black and white) children whose families were "passing" (counting themselves as white), and were allowed to do so by the white Cubans and the white American and Italian community, which had now begun to develop power in the governance of Tampa.

On Colored Children's Day, the succeeding day, black children could enter free of charge, and the two black ghettoes would empty of children early in the morning. Eager with anticipation of our fun fest, for which we had been saving coins for weeks, we swarmed by the thousands to the fair. We waited impatiently for an hour or so until the gates opened.

During the wait, a babble of voices would be talking and yelling to friends:

"I'm going to head for the flying planes."

"For me it will be the electric bumping cars."

"I'll take the giant merry-go-round."

"Food, food, food, that's what I want first, a jumbo hot dog and a coke."

"I'm not going to see the exhibits until I've done my first round of rides."

Perhaps, I hoped secretly, I would have one ride with Verdell, the unrequited love of my childhood. I followed her discreetly for a twenty yards or so, but she was obviously ignoring me. So, in defeat, I withdrew from the chase. I now realize that Verdell was a child of mixed Cuban and American parentage. Her father, a black Cuban, and her mother, a black American, was divorced when Verdell was very young. Though Verdell lived in the Cuban ghetto, she had none of her activities within it. Assuming her mother's identity, she attended a Protestant church and had her social life within the black American ghetto. She was comfortable and very popular as a black American beauty, the rage among black American boys older than I was. I believe that she considered me childish and immature. She was right.

So I spent my time at the fair in the company of young boys. We roamed the fair grounds like adolescent bull elephants, waiting for the maturity and the strength to compete for females. We had fun, but not as much as the boys who had dates. When not so engaged, I became the millstone around my sister Sylvia's neck, impeding her flirtations and fun with boys. That suited mother just fine. She listened to Sylvia's complaints about me with little or no sympathy.

Social class, different languages, and different cultures divided the two communities. Black Cubans still built dependent relationships with black Americans, especially our black American teachers, with whom we formed deep, affectionate bonds. But we lived clearly on the margins of black American society, while we worked out our daily existence in the black Cuban ghetto in Ybor City. Yet, our identity as black Americans developed strongly. I remember but one black Cuban hero, Antonio Maceo, the general who had led the fight for Cuba's independence from Spain. There were no photographs in my home of historically significant Cuban blacks.

My heart and mind belonged to Nat Turner, Frederick Douglass, Harriet Tubman, Sojourner Truth, Paul Laurence Dunbar, John Brown, Paul Robeson, Langston Hughes, W. E. B. Dubois, Allison Davis, Alain Locke, and the two brothers, James Weldon and James Rosamond Johnson, who wrote the song very dear to my heart, "Lift Every Voice and Sing."

CHAPTER 4

Mother

THE ALARM SOUNDED at 5:30 A.M. She got out of bed immediately to attend to the many chores that faced a widow of thirty-six with five children: washing, ironing, and mending the clothes we were to wear to school, soaking the beans for the evening meal, making the coffee. Already her face had the look of resolution.

Beautiful, very agile, and very smart, she moved rapidly, tending to the chores, sometimes two and three at once. Seldom graced by a smile, her face reflected resignation to a difficult, somewhat onerous obligation.

By 6:30 we began to stir and to ready ourselves for the daily litany of instructions, warnings, and advice she gave us:

"Be sure to wear clean underwear, for you never know when you will have an accident requiring that you take your clothes off, exposing your dirty drawers. If you haven't changed them, that would be a disgrace.

"Leave the kitchen spotless with everything in its place. Then, if you are brought home ill or hurt, whoever is helping you will be able to find things needed, like a pot for boiling water.

"Listen carefully to your teachers. Do what they ask you to do. I would be so ashamed if a complaint about any of you came from school, that I would not be able to face the world. [*This implied, as she frequently did, that she would harm herself in some way.*]

"Sylvia, start the beans as soon as you come home from school so that they will be done when I return from work. Start the rice at five o'clock.

"Don't let me hear from the neighbors that there has been fighting among you. Don't tell me who was right and who was wrong. You will have brought shame upon the house, and I'll punish both of you."

All of our talk with Mother was carried out in Spanish, the language of our home. While she was giving us our charge, she was completing her toilet, donning a freshly ironed dress, and arranging her long hair into an attractive, neat bun.

Tall, thin, erect, she walked out of the house and headed for the cigar factory, twenty minutes away. She strode resolutely down the street towards the cigar factory, where she labored until five-thirty in the afternoon.

After she left, we scurried around the house getting ready for school, fixing our bologna sandwiches, eating buttered bread and drinking *cafe con leche* (coffee with milk), our daily breakfast. We gave the house a quick once-over to make it ready for the hypothetical stranger who might bring us home sick or injured.

Before I was old enough to go to school, I walked daily through the back yard, across the alley, to Mrs. Byna's house. An ancient, large, unpainted, and weathered duplex, it sat alone on the half-block of lots which, in the past, must have held a number of its counterparts. It was the lone survivor of a family of dinosaurs that gradually was dying out. Silhouetted against the eastern sky in the morning, Mrs. Byna's was the very model of a haunted house, complete with myriad bats that inhabited its attic.

In the evening, just at the deepest dusk between gray day and black night fell, the bats would emerge from the attic, forming an immense cloud as they flew out to find their nightly feast of mosquitoes. Their individual chirps would blend into one sustained whistle, loud, shrill, and eerie, gradually diminishing as the cloud disappeared into the distance. Just as predictably, the swarms would return at that precise moment when night becomes dawn.

During the day, tiny flakes of bat guano shimmered in the bright sunlight as they descended onto the furniture, the beds, the floor, the lamps, onto everything in their path. The guano lent an acrid smell to the house. Mrs. Byna swept and dusted everything daily; else the bat dust would collect in layers of fine red powder. I was very aware of it when I was eating the soup and sandwich that Mrs. Byna fed me every noon, just before I took my sternly enforced nap.

The only black American neighbor who lived in a home close to ours, Mrs. Byna became my mother's good friend. A stout woman of about sixty, she gave me kind and caring love, though she very firmly insisted that I take my daily nap. I felt safe and secure with Mrs. Byna. I could feel her great affection for me. Her eyes were soft when she spoke to me. She often placed me on her lap and gave me warm hugs.

Not once did she strike me, even lightly. She read to me daily and she helped me to read to her. I would have enjoyed having my mother treat me with the tenderness that Mrs. Byna demonstrated. Somehow I knew that my mother loved me; she just couldn't express herself physically.

After Mrs. Byna's home was condemned and demolished, I visited her almost daily on my way back from school, at her new house, about six blocks deeper into the black American ghetto. She helped me to develop a strong identity with black Americans. She was crucial, I believe, to my development of a sense of being loved by adults.

The last house having been removed, the boys in the neighborhood now had a half-block of land on which to play baseball, about which the entire town was passionate. The larger and bigger boys, dreaming of major-league careers, played the game seriously and well enough to attract large crowds of older men returning from work. These men took up collections to keep the teams supplied with balls, bats, gloves, and other equipment. Knowing how strict my mother was with me, the boys found a spot as batboy for me, thus legitimating my status and allaying my mother's fears, which she frequently expressed, that I would be hurt.

Mother worked in the cigar factory five and one-half days a week as one of the *boncheras,* the women who bunched the fillers of the cigars with good but rough tobacco, before the cigars went into the wooden molds to be firmly pressed into shape and passed on to the master craftsmen for finishing. She was paid very little.

As I grew older, it became my task during the summers to take my mother a lunch, prepared by Sylvia, usually of leftovers from the previous evening's meal. A hot meal, if at all possible, was an imperative. We had a four-tiered enamelware lunch carrier for transporting hot meals, sometimes only rice and fried eggs. We ate rice at every meal. In a pinch, fried eggs filled in very nicely to complete a meal. We did not eat green vegetables other than salad greens, cabbage, and string beans. But we ate large quantities of bananas, oranges, grapefruit, tangerines, and mangos.

The lunch trip became an adventure. Eating would be over quickly. Then, Mother took the opportunity to introduce me to her fellow workers. "This is my baby, Evelio. He is a fine boy. I am very proud of him," she told them.

She would let me peek into the factory at the long tables, arranged in rows, where the cigar makers worked. If I tarried a little, after they had resumed work, I even could hear the slap of their *chavetas,* or knives, as they put them down over and over in the course of shaping cigars. The *chavetas* were broad, about four inches long and two inches wide, with a rounded blade that permitted the workers to use a rolling, rather than a slicing, motion in cutting the tobacco leaf. The highly regarded master *tabaqueros* practically sculpted the cigars into exact replicas one of the others with their fingers and their *chavetas.*

I became familiar with the aristocrat of the cigar-making industry, the *lector* or reader, chosen for his erudition, his command of the language, and his ability to read with dramatic fervor. Chosen by the workers, he received his pay individually from the workers themselves. At fifteen cents per worker per week, that came to more than thirty dollars a week—handsome pay indeed. The black Cuban community was very proud of the only black *lector,* Facundo Accion, who carried himself with great dignity. He was, without question, the black Cuban community's recognized leading intellectual.

Perched on a platform above the tables where the cigar makers worked, the lector read the newspaper from cover to cover in the morning: news, features, sports, business. Then, from two to four in the afternoon, he brought alive a great novel.

Les Miserables was the novel I remember most vividly, because of the enthusiastic discussion it generated among my mother and her fellow workers. "What would you do? Faced with the starvation of your children, what would you do?" became the question asked often by one neighbor or the other. They all seemed stumped by Hugo's skillfully posed dilemma.

I listened with great interest to daily discussions of the developments in Jean Valjean's life as woven by Hugo in his masterpiece. Cervantes' *Don Quixote* drew great attention also.

Mother had delegated to Sylvia full responsibility for the cleanliness of the house and for starting the evening meal. She also gave Sylvia full hegemony over me. Even now, Mother's serious face stands out vividly, admonishing me: "Evelio, you must mind Sylvia. Do what she tells you to do. Help her to keep the house clean." Sylvia had, in effect, the responsibility for mothering me, monitoring my movements, accompanying me to school and back, and making all the arrangements that school required.

My brothers would bribe her with a dime or fifteen cents to do their share of the chores. In turn, she promptly bribed me with a lesser share. The bribe, and the prospect of being in her good graces, provided more than enough incentive to make me a willing participant in the fraud.

Sylvia bore the brunt of the work, for mother depended upon her heavily for help in running the house. My three brothers, Henry, Raúl, and Aníval, were each assigned two large rooms to keep clean and orderly. Sylvia's domain was the kitchen and the laundry room. My jobs were to keep the front and back porches clean and to rake the yards so that the sand would look neat.

Sylvia, using the power that mother had given her, made my life very difficult. We fought frequently. Yet she always took good physical care of me, seeing to it that I ate and supervising my dressing. Four years older than I, much taller and heavier, she was a strong big sister to have around when, as sometimes happened, some schoolmate threatened me.

A marked change in our relationship came about when, at one point, I had endured enough of her bullying. She had long lorded it over me unmercifully, like some feudal potentate, in front of the girls who lived next door, with one of whom I was secretly in love.

"*Evelio,*" she addressed me imperiously that day, and asked me to bring her something or the other. Then, as though to demonstrate her dominion over me, she gave me a slight slap. .

Embarrassed, ashamed, and furious, I ran into the back yard, found a board of sufficient thickness and length, and rushed back into the house screaming, "*Abusadora! Abusadora!*" (Abuser! Abuser!) With all my might I swung the board and brought it down full force on the back of her thigh, exposed as she lay on her stomach. The board made a thick welt: beautiful, fully expressive of my rage.

Sylvia arose in surprise and shock. Yet I believe she admired me for my reaction. She also may have become aware of the enormity of her mistreatment of me and apprehensive of mother's reaction once she knew the facts, for Mrs. Byna came over and took me back to her house to await my mother's return from work.

Sylvia never slapped me again. As the years passed, we became good friends, in keeping with the many years we spent together, just the two of us, in the house on Eighth Avenue.

Of our brood, the eldest was Henry, who was twelve when our father died. Raúl, Aníval, and Sylvia followed, in approximately eighteen-month intervals. I was the youngest, three years and ten months old at the death of my father.

I remember being in the house on Eighth Avenue and having a thoroughly miserable time of it, as my mother assumed total responsibility for our rearing.

Henry went to Cuba to learn to be a barber. Raúl got a job as a delivery boy for a large store downtown. Al (as we called Aníval) somehow became connected to the parish, and ran errands for the priest in the Model A Ford the priest owned.

Mother would return at 5:45, her dress wrinkled, soiled, and reeking of tobacco. She would have an air of weariness as she walked into the house and sat down in the living room to receive the daily report from Sylvia, and, as I grew older, from me.

"What did you do today" How long did you practice the piano? How did it go at school?" She always looked piercingly into our eyes, to discern if we were telling the truth. Her imposing figure dominated us.

"We did fine, Mamá," Sylvia replied carefully, for Mother's wrath was awesome when aroused and we did not risk arousing it often. I had the role of "substantiator," else I was subject to Sylvia's wrath, itself formidable.

No levity accompanied these exchanges. Mother was a stern, strong-willed woman, and humor had no place among her techniques for handling her brood. She was very serious, very hard-working, very dedicated to our upbringing, and very scrupulous.

The community respected her highly. It admired her for the determination with which she managed her home and reared her children while working full-time. They were not, however, fully supportive of the rigid, extreme control she exercised over us and the ways by which she maintained it, including restricting us to the house, forbidding us to play with other children, and threatening to harm herself if we did not behave.

"*I am going to hang myself from a telephone pole!*" she would scream at us when we had driven her to distraction. At times she would literally pull wisps of her hair out, to demonstrate her exasperation over something we had done or not done.

Tired as she must have been, she terminated these interrogations in short order. Rapidly removing her work clothes, then washing her hands and face, she quickly went about preparing the evening meal. Sylvia and I faced Mother with mixed feelings, apprehensive in giving the account of the day, yet pleased because we anticipated Mother's finishing the meal for which Sylvia had cooked the rice, a routine followed daily.

And excellent meals they were! Chicken stewed in a light tomato sauce, wonderfully seasoned; fish, marinated in lemon juice and garlic before being broiled, or baked; the great soups, garbanzo beans with cabbage and pig knuckles, for example; the rice, perfectly cooked with every grain separate, the beans, now given her special touch with olive oil and an array of spices; and always a salad, rich with lettuce, and cooked string beans, avocado, and tomatoes.

I now understand the influence of her example of hard work: those meals, her meticulous housekeeping, her insistence that our clothes be always clean and ironed, however old they might be. All of these played a role in developing us into well-behaved children. But a large measure of our conformity she achieved through her strong will and the strong measures by which she enforced it.

In the perspective of years I have been able to understand her with less resentment of her stern demeanor. She had no one to talk to intimately, no one to help assuage her pain and weariness, no one to make love to her.

Deep down, she must have resented us to some degree. Our care absorbed every moment of her day and every bit of her energy. I remember few instances when she did something for herself, like going to a neighbor's house to visit. Her only dress-up occasions were her infrequent visits to the school to see us perform, and the baptisms, weddings, and funerals that were part of our community life.

In her own fashion she was lovable but unloved, the severity of her demeanor toward us as children affecting our compassion as we watched her work so hard in caring for us. I now ask myself, "Did I let her know that I loved her?" Beneficiaries of her wisdom and her strength, we learned the meaning of tenacity. She set high standards for our behavior. She insisted, for example, that each of us take music lessons. Henry and Sylvia learned to play the piano passably. Raúl became an excellent violinist.

We were high achievers in school. Fortunate to have high expectations set for us, all five of us attended college. Three of us earned professional degrees beyond college, surpassing by quantums Mother's all-consuming goal: keeping us out of jail!

I remember her, her face distorted by determination, saying often, "No child of mine will ever go to jail," implying horrible consequences for any of us who breached her codes. Strangulation seemed an option she might well choose if a policeman ever should appear at our door.

My brother Henry returned from Cuba. Thin, awkward, and red-faced, he reflected the pain and the confusion inherent in his changed relationship to our mother. I believe that, of all of the children, he paid the highest price as a result of the death of our father. He obviously had suffered a great deal in Cuba. He returned as a fine barber, but as a very bitter and confused adolescent. I believe that he was given the rough treatment and arduous tasks which seemed to be the lot of apprentices. He left Tampa very quickly. Somehow he attended Bethune Cookman College in Daytona Beach, Florida for a year or two and, eventually, he settled in Washington, D.C.

He became very close to Mary McCloud Bethune while at Bethune Cookman, When she came to Washington, D.C., to serve in the National Youth Administration, he was one of the volunteers Mrs. Bethune relied upon to help her carry out her extensive public relations obligations.

Raúl had set his mind on becoming a mortician. He landed a job in a Jacksonville mortuary. But soon he returned home, the family's second victim of tuberculosis. After two or so years of attempting to arrest the course of the disease by bed rest at home, Mother sent him to Cuba, where medical care for blacks was vastly superior to that available in Tampa.

I never saw him again. He died in Cuba in 1934, at the age of twenty-one. I remember Raúl for his gracious good humor. He would make Sylvia and me laugh with his jokes and pranks. He was an excellent violinist, who never had to be exhorted or cajoled to practice. Whenever I hear the piece "Souvenir" I think of Raúl, about whom I don't have a single unhappy memory. He really understood that one has to make it oneself, and he clearly prepared himself for success. Even while he was at home undergoing the interminable hours of bed rest, he never showed impatience or overbearing behavior to Sylvia or me. He supervised his own care so as to expose us minimally. How I longed to hug him! He never let us get close to him.

Our stepfather Luis came to live with us after the Great Depression had descended. A thin man of about five feet six inches, he was the classic passive observer. He spoke no English and was totally lost outside the black Cuban ghetto. He gave my mother little help. Clearly one of the Depression's victims, he never found work again, except for an occasional odd job.

A thoroughly defeated and humorless man, he played no direct role in my upbringing, though he did play an indirect role in my sex education. I had very few notions about how the sex act was carried out. By sleeping with my mother, Luis taught me a few helpful, exciting lessons. Together, they made intriguing noises, poorly contained by the thin walls. Once, I mustered the courage to peep through the keyhole into the bedroom. I saw them carry out amazing gyrations under the blanket. I was wild with excitement, afraid of being caught, and guilty, because I knew I was doing something wrong.

Another experience informed me. During the hot summers I would spend an occasional day at my grandmother's house. She lived on Ninth Avenue in about the same position that our house occupied on Eighth Avenue. I had simply to walk across the street and duck between two neighbors' houses, and I would be at Grandmother's back doorstep. Since I did not have much room to roam, two neighborhood girls who lived across the street from me came to play with me.

One of them, about thirteen years old, and not only older but bolder, sat on the floor to take her turn at jacks. She sat in such a manner as to expose fully her pubic region to me through her torn panties. Excitement overwhelmed me as I stared with impunity at her private parts. Her intent was clear: to give me a good view. I trembled and sweated with guilt, but, as I remember the experience, I kept looking.

On the succeeding Saturday, I rushed to church to go to confession, burst into the confession box and blurted out, "Forgive me, Father, for I have sinned. I have committed adultery." I don't know whether the priest was amused or annoyed. My objective, however, was achieved: to relieve my guilt.

I never knew when or where Mother married Luis, but by way of establishing his right to be in the house and to sleep with her, Mother called us aside one day and solemnly showed us a marriage certificate.

During those years on Eighth Avenue, between roughly my fourth and tenth birthdays, we lived as a family in what must have been a typical house. The houses on our block, all identical, stood very close to one another, about four feet apart. They may have been about five to six hundred square feet in area. They were either unpainted or had not been painted in years. They sat on brick pilings, about four feet off the ground.

The roof, built of corrugated tin sheets, had no insulation between it and the ceilings of the rooms below it. A strong rain made a great noise, sheer excitement for me.

We did have the luxury of a flush toilet, located in a far corner of the back yard. Too afraid to use it at night, we resorted to the usual bucket for our needs after dark.

We bathed in a large tin tub set in the middle of the kitchen, the water heated in buckets on the stove. The rooms were heated with kerosene stoves. These were fitted with wicks, which, when lighted, heated a round chamber from which the heat radiated and warmed the air. We carried the heaters from the bedrooms to the dining rooms and back, for it was in those rooms that we spent most of our time once winter descended.

We must have been very poor at that time, but I don't remember *feeling* poor until we moved out of the house on Eighth Avenue to the house on Sixth Avenue, to accommodate Raúl's need for a large airy room in which to take his bed rest.

That lasted only about a year. Mother, determining that she could not afford the rent of six dollars a week, moved us to Thirteenth Avenue, above Twenty-second Street, into the top unit of a ramshackle triplex which had a porch so that Raúl could sleep outside.

While we lived on Eighth Avenue, Sylvia and I waged our relentless battle against roaches, rats and bedbugs every Saturday. We scrubbed every floor with Octagon soap, a very strong soap of the day. The floors gleamed bright yellow upon drying. The linoleum carpets—we never had a rug—were washed and polished. Every drawer was emptied and aired, to prevent roach infestation. Every bed was stripped, the mattresses and springs taken out to the back yard to lie in the sun throughout the day. We inserted newspapers between the coils of the springs, and then we set fire to the newspapers, thus destroying the bedbugs and their eggs. As the bugs scurried to the outside surface of the coils, they would be fried in the flames. The really big ones, gorged from their human feasts, would burst with a popping sound, yielding the acrid smell of boiling blood.

Every stitch of soiled clothes was washed and ironed. We did not overlook a cranny or a crevice, else we had to face the considerable ire of Mother, whose preferred method of punishment was to hit us on the head with the heel of her shoe.

We knew we had completed our work when, about four o'clock in the afternoon, I would rake the front and back yards, and Sylvia would start cooking the usual pot of rice. Then we bathed and dressed in clean clothes, and waited for Mother, who inspected our work in a manner akin to that of an army first sergeant.

Mother would arrive with the meat or fish for the evening meal. If she was pleased by the results she saw, she gave us a few coins to spend on Seventh Avenue, that most wonderful of streets!

CHAPTER 5

Seventh Avenue

SEVENTH AVENUE SEEMED LIKE A COUNTY FAIR every day, but especially so on Saturdays. When I walk along its ten blocks of activity now, I wonder how I could have thought it so long, so wide, so utterly beautiful and enchanting. Sylvia and I would walk out the back gate, across the large empty lot where once Mrs. Byna's house stood, to Seventh Avenue, that marvel of things to buy, if one had money, or simply to see and enjoy, if one had none. We walked briskly and excitedly, for this was Saturday afternoon, all the chores were completed, and we had hard-earned permission from Mother to walk up and down the street.

Its Old World charm, wrought-iron balconies over sidewalks, and large-European-style buildings that housed the social clubs, were all wasted on us. We were too excited about spending our money!

"Let's hurry," Sylvia would press. "We can make it all the way to Twentieth Street and back before dark, if we try."

"Okay, but I want to spend some time in the stores to see if we can find something to buy," I responded, eager to spend my coins.

Ever the one in charge, Sylvia nodded graciously and said, "We'll see."

The years immediately following Father's death found my family in such narrow straits financially, that a "looking" trip and a "shopping" trip yielded almost equal pleasure. They both gave us something exciting to do!

Across Twelfth Street, we stole glances, through swinging half-doors, into the formidable café whence the *bolita* numbers emerged every day except Sunday. Next door, Ramo's Meat Market stood proudly as one of the last large-scale retail enterprises still in the hands of white Cubans.

Across the street, some Italians owned a large fish market. With her meager budget mother purchased Gulf of Mexico red snapper, and the incomparable *serrucho,* the sawfish, known to some Americans as Spanish mackerel and to others as kingfish. I had no idea until years later that these were delicacies, held in high esteem today by gourmets.

Walking further up the street we passed some residences which anachronistically remained in the middle of this now-commercial block. Verdell, my unrequited secret love, lived in one of these houses. Sometimes, I would catch a glimpse of her. Sometimes, even, I would get to say a few hurried embarrassed sentences to her. She would flash her incomparable, deeply dimpled smile. That was as much as I could bear. I would walk away in total confusion and joy almost intolerable.

Sylvia would tease, "So you saw Dreamboat herself?"

I remained silent, in flushed embarrassment, yet happy to have seen Verdell, on whom I had a devastating crush.

Past Thirteenth Street, the produce markets thrived, with fruits and vegetables cascading in luscious abundance on either side of the aisles. We could spend one of our pennies there, for a banana or a tangerine. Going beyond, to Fourteenth and Fifteenth streets, the dry-goods stores, the furniture store and the fine men's wear store huddled together as though they found comfort in each other.

Mother bought me my first suit with long pants in the men's wear store. With the Depression in full swing, she could not afford it, as the sad look and deep sigh with which she accepted the salesman's final offer clearly showed.

Nearby, and on the same side of the street stood S. H. Kress Co., the "expensive" five- and ten-cent store. We never went into it. Most of its prices exceeded our means by twenty cents or a quarter.

We clutched our coins tightly until we arrived at Woolworth's, our very own paradise, where we could turn nickels and pennies into trinkets, adornments for the hair, or, perhaps, a handkerchief. It seems to me that we always bought combs, for sales on combs could always be found. Always some could be bought for a penny.

Moving farther up to Eighteenth Street we passed all the forbidden places: the elegant and famous Las Novedades Restaurant, where waiters all suited up in tuxedos tossed veritable snowstorms of white tablecloths around. Totally fascinated, I watched the patrons come and go, not understanding how one could become wealthy enough to afford to dine in a place so special.

Then we would pass the clubs: on Twentieth Street the Italian Club, where people hurried in and out preparing for the night's festivities; and the Asturian (Spanish) Club, which seemed more subdued. The Asturians also had a large building and an elaborate program. The Asturians puzzled me because I could not place them. I was in college before I learned that they came from Asturias, a province in Spain.

I always felt strange when I passed the Cuban movie theater. I could not attend it. But some cousins who were light enough to "pass" attended the movie house weekly. Their darker brothers never even tried to seek admission.

The businesses that did not sell goods were located above Twentieth Street: the banks, the post office, a storefront cigar-making shop very popular with tourists, an insurance office, and the like.

These weekly forays took place in the summer, while there was still light in the early evenings. We would scurry back before dusk, with our spirits high and our bodies loaded down with our loot, such as it was. Much in the tradition of children everywhere and in all times, we had had a wonderful time, whatever the world may have thought of our relative penury. To be sure, we had much to enjoy: food, clothing, health, school, church, a warm and secure home, and the fun of Seventh Avenue.

The Depression that followed the Crash of 1929 threatened all of these. It slowly closed most doors and, like a blanket, covered everything we had known as secure. It seemed as though some powerful hand had slowly turned out the lights on our beautiful Seventh Avenue.

CHAPTER 6

Noche Buena: The Good Night

TURKEY DINNERS, so important to and symbolic of the American celebrations of Thanksgiving and Christmas, defined my youth. My American schoolmates spoke enthusiastically about turkey, especially at the holidays. I had no part in those discussions.

My circle of school friends included Bill Dawkins and Michael and Robert Wilson. We were about twelve at the time. Michael and Robert, whose family considered itself to be the first family of the parish, always had an effusive description of their turkey.

"My father ordered a twenty-six pound turkey yesterday," Michael boasted.

"Yeah, we're going to have some friends over for Thanksgiving," Robert added.

Bill, a very much more a regular guy, and more low-key, said something like, "We're going to Grandma's house."

But I did not know turkey in my home. I did not understand the concept of "all the trimmings." Particularly at Thanksgiving, I had no way of participating in these happy, excited discussions.

My family did not celebrate Thanksgiving. A purely American holiday, Thanksgiving did not mix with the traditions my parents brought from Cuba. We had no comparable and concurrent festivity to discuss while our American friends had all that fun looking forward to Thanksgiving.

A subdued mood descended upon Cuban children at Thanksgiving. We did not dislike it exactly; but we did not welcome it either, for it intensified our feelings of being different and odd. We had only an ordinary meal, while our friends had great celebrations of food, family, church, and community.

Christmas was a different experience. Although we could not participate in all that turkey talk, our feelings of strangeness were mitigated by our anticipation of own special kind of Christmas.

31

Our celebration of Christmas resembled the American way, but at the same time it differed substantially. We looked forward to toys, and gifts, to attendance at church and family gatherings. We participated fully in school festivities and church celebrations. We went to midnight Mass and sang the traditional songs, mostly in Latin. They included the great, joyful Gloria; the solemn, ponderous Credo; and the passionate Agnus Dei, the Lamb of God to whom we pled for mercy and peace. We also sang songs in English. My favorites were "O! Holy Night," "Angels We Have Heard On High," and "Go Tell It on the Mountain."

Much of our celebration and our food differed completely. We celebrated Christmas Eve, not Christmas Day. and we called it Noche Buena, the "Good Night." Christmas Day was anticlimactic. We looked forward to Christmas Eve, to Noche Buena, a celebration of family, friendship, church, and community.

Late in the evening, we gathered in the home of one or the other of a group of families which knew one another well. The centerpiece of the feast was *lechón*, baked pig, succulent and crispy, a delicacy we thought worth the long wait from one Christmas Eve to the next.

Mother dressed the pig—rubbed with salt, painted with crushed garlic, drenched in lemon juice, and sprinkled with spices—in an enormous baking pan borrowed from a local baker, to whom we took the pig early on the morning of Christmas Eve to be baked in the huge ovens. When we called for the pig in the late afternoon, we met other families that had brought their pigs to the same baker.

I remember most vividly a Christmas Eve before the Depression. Everyone was employed, so we did not have to skimp on food, clothes, and heat. My mother did not take the pig to the bakery this time. Rather, Antonio, a middle-aged relative who lived with us, fashioned a grate upon which a pig, weighing about forty pounds, sizzled and smoked as it roasted over a bed of charcoal. My mother gave me the enormously important responsibility, I thought, of basting the pig with a mixture of lemon juice and finely crushed garlic as it cooked slowly throughout the day.

I took the task very seriously, basting the pig over and over with a paintbrush dipped into the bowl of lemon juice and garlic. I also monitored the fire under the pig, telling Antonio when it needed additional charcoal.

Meanwhile, in the kitchen, elaborate additional preparations went on for the feast. Friends arrived with their contributions: baked chickens, cakes, pies, a large pot of black beans, and fixings for the salad—lettuce, tomatoes, cucumbers, and avocados.

My mother did not bake bread, and I don't remember the smells of baking bread in any of the kitchens with which I was familiar. At every meal, we ate Cuban bread, provided by the ubiquitous small bakeries. Narrower and shorter than French bread, it has the same form and texture. The loaves looked like baguettes, only they were somewhat wider and thicker. We topped the feast with *turrón,* a very rich almond confection imported from Spain. This was eaten only at Christmas, for it cost a pretty penny.

Home-made raisin wine accompanied the meal. Mother fermented the wine in five-gallon crockery containers. When it was ready, she siphoned it into one-gallon jugs. She made the wine one year for the next. We buried the seven or eight gallons she made in the back yard about two feet under ground; at the same time, we uncovered the previous year's batch. I believe Mother buried the wine not only to age it under the cool ground, but also because, under Prohibition, having wine in the house may have been risky. The yearly digging up of the old wine and burial of the new became a tradition and a ceremony in which the entire household participated.

Our house was small; it hardly accommodated the number of people who attended the feast and party. So we moved all the furniture, except the table and the chairs, to the bedrooms and to the back porch. The table, extended with four inserted leaves, left only enough room for diners to circle it. When it was finally set, at about nine-thirty in the evening, my child's eyes glowed with delight at the beautiful feast.

A large platter of crisply roasted pig was placed in the center, and a platter of baked chicken at each end. Bowls of black beans and string beans, platters of saffron (yellow rice) laced with strips of pimentos, and other platters of fried plantains, were placed between. Two large platters of colorful salad at each end completed the scene. I stood transfixed and excruciatingly excited by the gaiety, the sheer beauty, of it all.

Then the serving and the eating began. We ate buffet style, the diners coming up to the table in random order and filling their plates, while remarking about the special excellence of this meal. The dining mood descended, with every one concentrating on the food. Bursts of laughter penetrated the room from time to time. I do not remember anything anyone said, but I remember vividly the noises of merriment and the room full of happy faces.

At about 11:15 the children would leave for midnight Mass. We joined friends who were on their way to mass also and we sang carols along the way. The church would be packed. We enjoyed tremendously the singing of High Mass, for which we had been practicing for nearly a month. After mass the entire congregation would gather in front of the church, greeting each other in the dark cold night. We returned to our homes singing carols to the top of our lungs, a thoroughly fulfilled group of very happy children.

Dancing to the tunes of a Victrola, an early version of the record player, had begun in the living room. The adults completely accepted the children into the circle of fun and festivities. We danced along with the adults, fully part of the group. Not limited to dancing with each other, we danced with anyone of the opposite gender. There were no patronizing remarks, and not even a hint of reluctance, as adults danced with us and helped us with the steps. Primarily, they concentrated on helping us with the rhythm and the beat. Once we swayed in unison with them, they praised us profusely with an "*Ay! Mira que lindo!*" (My! How handsome you are!)

My very favorite dancing partner was Lola, also called La Filipina or The Philippine Lady. She and her mother were my mother's best friends. Her mother, Nena, was my godmother. My aunt Gloria, and my cousin, Carmelina, were my two other special dance partners.

Lola's was one of the two homes I could visit without special permission from my mother, and where I was free to stay for dinner. If I was not in the house when mother arrived from work, she would assume that I was at Lola's or at Aunt Gloria's house.

A plump mother of seven children, Lola had a beaming smile that lighted my life always. Thirty-five or so years of age, she furnished her house sparsely with wooden chairs and tables. She had six boys and just one girl, so fancier furnishings probably would not have taken the punishment. I went frequently to her house, a haven of peace for me, to escape the rigidities and the exhortations of my mother.

Lola had married Willie, a black American. Although theirs was an Americanized family, it retained much of Cuban culture. Their cuisine, drawing from both Cuban and black American traditions, made their table a delight for stragglers like me. I learned to eat hamhocks, collard greens, and black-eyed peas at Lola's house.

Lola loved me and she let me know it. I can still feel the warmth of her mountainous breasts as she held me in a tight hug. I believe that she knew she sometimes harbored me from the severe atmosphere and lack of intimacy my mother generated in our home. With her great capacity to love and her inexhaustible good humor, she captivated me. I felt safe and secure, and very happy whenever I was in her presence.

Lola danced with me as though I were an eminently able partner, beaming, laughing and subtly guiding me into leading her. I must have been about eleven years old at the time. I still flash back to the happy times Lola made possible for me.

I went to sleep at about two o'clock in the morning. When I awoke, at about six, the house was completely in order, the kitchen cleaned, and the furniture all rearranged. The Christmas tree, decorated, as usual, on Christmas Eve, would be glowing in a corner of the living room. Our one present each would be displayed under the tree—a shiny pair of skates the one I recall most vividly.

On Christmas Day a subdued, almost quiet, mood descended over the neighborhood. The adults rested. The children played outside with whatever toy each had received. There was no cooking, and no sit-down meal. We simply picked at the food left from the Noche Buena feast.

If there was ever a time in my life when I felt sublimely happy, this was it. Home, family, community, school, and church all played their roles with maximum effectiveness. They were all exquisitely happy places to be, and I was the fortunate beneficiary of all this love.

PART TWO

Going Up North

CHAPTER 7

Tally Wop

THE AMERICAN PATTERN of rigid segregation of blacks and whites asserted itself in the schools with unrestrained, brutal vigor. For all of our sharing of language, culture, and religion with white Cubans, we black Cubans were black. When the school bell rang, we joined the streams of children headed toward the "colored" schools. School resolved all of my confusion about my color, my Spanish tongue, and my culture. I was a black boy. *That's* what was important!

We attended St. Peter Claver's, a Catholic school for blacks, located two blocks on the "other" side of Nebraska Avenue, the psychological boundary between the black American and black Cuban ghettoes. While some black Americans lived in Ybor City, no black Cubans lived outside Ybor City and West Tampa, across the river in a barely developed section of the city.

We walked to school in groups, as have children in all places and at all times, seeking the opportunity to socialize with friends and protection from threats, imagined or real. A very small part of the student body, we black Cubans spoke Spanish, and that set us apart, and made us subject to the derision which all language minorities experience in all societies.

When they wanted to tease us, our black American schoolmates called us *tally wops*. That phrase, a combination of two slang terms applied to Italians, rang out in the schoolyard whenever black Cuban children were being addressed derisively. Our schoolmates found it difficult to distinguish between the Spanish and Italian languages, so since we sounded Italian to their ears, they attached the misnomers to us. At any rate, the mean and combative black American students called us *tally wop* in loud and jeering voices and with great delight. They never physically abused us, but they did substantial hurt to our feelings.

For the Grillos, they had an additional torture. The name Grillo, in translation, means cricket, or grasshopper. So we carried a double burden. We frequently heard the call, "Hey, *grasshopper!* You TALLY WOP!"

In the main, nonetheless, we had very positive feelings about the school experience. We were fully integrated with our black American schoolmates. We were blacks, subsumed for all purposes within a monolithic group.

Within this amalgam we were introduced to the rich culture and heritage of black America. The great black churches, which we did not enter, but whose rich pageantry of people we were able to observe and admire; the sense that opportunities for participation in group activities for youth were numerous; the great Negro newspapers, including our own weekly, *The Tampa Bulletin;* the sense of connectedness to the nation, nurtured by the frequent visit to our city of dignitaries, highly visible and distinguished officials of associations or famous scholars from the black colleges; above all, the many good and kind friends we made, the girls and boys we played with, fell in love with, and in a large number of cases, married, and, over the years, the sense of community that developed, the bonds that grew of our common condition, our common lot.

Those black Cubans who went to public schools had one advantage over those of us who went to parochial schools: They were much better grounded in black history.

Mirta, the daughter of two very black Cubans, a full generation older than my parents, and the only black Cuban college graduate I knew, had integrated herself completely into black American circles. The only black Cuban teacher in the public schools, Mirta held herself completely aloof from black Cubans. She found herself a niche within the circle of middle-class black Americans. wherein she had her social life.

She was a pioneer, teaching by her example that the future of black Cuban youth lay in integration with black Americans. Nonetheless, she seemed to me to have had limited contact with black Cubans. We never took umbrage, for we did not experience it as aloofness. Mirta was smart and educated highly and we were proud of her. Although we lived only two doors apart, I never entered their home.

Francisco, my contemporary, frequently had a black American schoolmate as visitor. That taught me that black Cuban children who attended the public schools had a much different experience from those who, like me, went to the Catholic school.

The parents did not speak English, but, nonetheless, they were the clearly the best educated of the black Cubans. I have the impression that the father, a superb orator, may have had higher education in Cuba. They were much more refined than were my family and the circles of which my family was part so, I believe that differences in our class statuses may have led to our perception of their social distance from us.

It is clear to me now that all of the children were destined for college. The two boys, both older than I, also became professionals, one an attorney, and later a minister, the other a highly placed professional in the music department of the black schools. They became solidly established as leaders of the black community. In retrospect, I now realize that they did not follow the black Cuban migration north. They returned to Tampa from college, to live a life of full integration with black Americans. I believe that they were Protestants, so their integration into the larger social group with which they identified was total.

As Catholics, black Cubans were isolated from the larger social group of white Catholics of which, in theory, we were a part. The whites with whom we did associate were all nuns and priests, missionaries.

Not a single conversation about college was ever held in my home. Nor were there any encyclopedias, novels, reference books, or magazines to arouse a child's imagination. No photographs, prints, or posters of heroic black Cubans graced our walls to teach us about our heritage.

I learned this when I entered the public high school in the tenth grade. There I was introduced to black history on a daily basis as we memorialized black heroes, or celebrated famous artists and scholars. Though not explicitly part of the curriculum, the history of slavery as dehumanizing seeped through the celebrations, the spirituals, the dramatic readings, and the way that the teachers treated us, the way they respected us precisely *because* we were black.

They seemed to want to steel us for the harsh experiences of living in a society that segregated us, to help us deal with the realities of discrimination in every aspect of the American society. The faculty was all black, and this distinguished them from the largely white faculties of the parochial schools.

At St. Peter Claver's we did celebrate a few significant historical events of special significance to blacks, such as the Emancipation Proclamation and President Lincoln's birthday. The line in the history books, as I remember it, had the slaves incapable of taking care of themselves.

Our walking-to-school groups always included a goodly number of black American children who lived in the Cuban ghetto, all, good friends and buddies, even. There also were children of mixed black Cuban and black American families, who usually took their primary identity from the black American mother. Thus, for example, the Garcias, whose father was a black Cuban and whose mother was a black American, spoke little Spanish in the home.

They cooked in the black American tradition, as we could tell by the lunches they brought to school. Ours invariably consisted of a bologna sandwich on sliced white bread and little else. The black American children had all kinds of interesting delicacies such as meat loaf, liverwurst, chicken, cornbread, a stick of celery, a small apple and, perhaps, a cookie or two. Occasionally, I would manage, with great satisfaction, to swap half of my bologna sandwich for half of a liverwurst sandwich. I could not imagine where my schoolmate's family could procure a delicacy so very special!

One day, a friend, Mason, led me across the street to the small grocery store where the pickle barrel always held hundreds of fat, juicy, delicious, pickles. "Here, buy one of these," he would entice. For a nickel, saved perhaps for weeks, I could buy one of these marvels, quite familiar to Mason but a rare treat for me. The entire experience was overlaid with a sense of adventure, for my mother would not have understood a sour pickle or a son who would risk her wrath to obtain one. Sensing my worry, Mason reassured, "Don't worry, your mother won't find out."

A patent missionary spirit pervaded St. Peter Claver's, named after a little-known black saint. Four white nuns, headed by the widely renowned and beloved Sister Felicity, were driven daily into the ghetto from the beautiful school where the Holy Names Sisters taught the children of rich whites along Tampa's famous Bayshore Boulevard.

This was heroic service indeed. The nuns who educated us did so by choice and, in every case, for many years. They showered us with love. They followed our progress with great pride in our accomplishments. They taught us superbly. They assured themselves that we had a good grasp of the written language. They provided rich opportunities for dramatic expression with plays or programs requiring the rigorous practice of the spoken language. Music was taught only in connection with religious celebrations. Instrumental music was not taught. The teaching of morals received the highest priority. Discipline was strict, but not harshly enforced. The sisters had their ways of praising, rewarding, setting high expectations, withholding small privileges, and instilling pride.

At the first ring of the bell, the schoolyard fell completely silent. Boys and girls lined up separately, folded their arms tightly, and waited until the clapper sounded before moving. We walked silently to our classrooms, stood by our desks, and sat down all together when the clapper sounded again.

Constantly stressing love, kindness, grace, and honesty, the nuns always warned us against stealing, lying, cursing, cheating, fighting, and thinking evil thoughts, speaking evil words, and engaging in evil actions. (The last three were euphemisms for sex, a forbidden subject of discussion.)

The catechism was taught by rote. The doctrines of Catholicism were taught in segments, which we repeated again and again. There was a routine followed with the Catechism, called "examination of conscience." There, sin was described and organized under each commandment to help us remember how, when, and where we had violated the laws of God and of the Church.

Thus, if we had disobeyed our parents or teachers, we had violated the commandment:

HONOR THY FATHER AND THY MOTHER.

If we had stolen anything, we had violated the commandment:

THOU SHALT NOT COVET THY NEIGHBOR'S GOODS.

Every lustful thought, feeling or deed offended

THOU SHALT NOT COMMIT ADULTERY.

We were taught that entering a Protestant church was sinful. I never did so until I left Tampa, except for attending the funeral of someone who was like family, Mrs. Bina's nephew. He had died from the long-term effects of gas poisoning in World War I. I must have been about twelve years old at the time.

Seeing a black minister preside over the funeral service and hearing him preach the sermon transfixed me. I was in another world. The minister was articulate and educated. He gave the congregation a dramatic history lesson about the origins of the First World War: How some member of royalty was assassinated in Sarajevo, and how others retaliated.

Waves of excitement coursed over me as he illuminated a critical part of our history, which had never been explained to me with such clarity and fervor. Eloquent and passionate, the minister held me rapt a uniquely emotional experience for me, and one far different from the bland homilies to which I had been accustomed from the priests at St. Peter's, who never discussed the immoralities of segregation and discrimination.

I know now that the nuns taught the children of the black middle class, the sons and daughters the dentist, the mortuary proprietor, and other small businessmen. Yet, despite its limited resources, the school accommodated a sizable group of students whose families (including my own) were not well off. The nuns exempted us from paying the fifty cents per week tuition when the Depression reduced the family to a marginal existence.

Despite their unreserved commitment to an excellent education for black children, despite the close and affectionate bonds they formed with us, there was one thing they could not teach us: the black culture. They could not help us understand our past as children of slaves, to handle the rage we harbored in the face of the inequities, the humiliations we faced on a daily basis in a totally segregated society. They could not help us to *feel* black.

We learned the story of Crispus Attucks when we studied the Revolutionary War. We learned about the Civil War. Homage was paid to Abraham Lincoln and to Booker T. Washington with bas-relief plaques attached to either side of the front of the building.

That about covered it. We did not sing Negro spirituals. Our recitations and dramatic programs never had black themes. We knew little of Frederick Douglass, Sojourner Truth, Phyllis Wheatley, Harriet Tubman, and Nat Turner. Praise was reserved for important figures such as the pope and the saints. Our black culture was subsumed, if not denied. In its place we were handed a European culture, complete with icons, heroes and heroines.

It never occurred to me that it could or should be otherwise. At the time, I accepted all of this as a matter of course. It is only from the perspective developed by living my adult life within the black American society that I am able to discern these important subtleties. The significant events in Tampa's black life took place in the big Baptist church across the street from the school and in the A.M.E. church on Harrison Street, and in other venues about which I knew absolutely nothing. I knew this because of the absence of communication about black American social life between my black American schoolmates and me.

I remember, for example, one long discussion about Boy Scouts held by a small group of schoolmates, all friends of mine. I remained silent throughout the entire conversation. What was a Boy Scout?

At that moment I felt isolated, as I have frequently, whenever I have confronted some aspect of black American life that was commonplace for my black American friends, but that seemed new and different and, even, strange for me. Similarly, I would sometimes give expression to something peculiarly Cuban with which my black American friends were unfamiliar. The quizzical looks, and sometimes, laughter, which followed left me feeling embarrassed, awkward, and very alone.

At Saint Peter Claver's only the first eight grades were taught. In the ninth grade we transferred to the public school, Booker T. Washington High School, a very crowded and difficult school, physically. The floors on the first story were made of rough concrete. The design did not provide for stairs in wells at the each end of the halls, as was customary. They were cut out of the hall itself, so that the halls would narrow to a passageway for only two columns of students, one going in one direction and the other in the opposite direction. Each change of classes was therefore strenuous, disheartening, and, to us, denigrating, an arrangement that had us perpetually resentful of the white administration.

Nonetheless, this school did make the subjects of slavery, of discrimination, and of prejudice palpable. The faculty of Booker Washington High fully confirmed our identity as black youth. Some great teachers provided the symbols and the ceremonies to support that identity. Franklin Harris, Jay Stewart, Miriam Anderson, and Mary White rank with the best teachers I have ever had. They encouraged and challenged us to resist the evils of a segregated society.

Mr. Harris, a tall, very handsome man, spoke to us forthrightly about America's evil racial policies. "Remember, you are our hope, and you must join the struggle to right these terrible wrongs," he would enjoin us. He was punished for being so outspoken.

Mrs. White had the role of the uplifter. The highly respected vice-principal, she did not get chummy with any of us. A model of dignity and self-respect, and a tremendous English teacher, her oft-repeated theme was: "Keep to the right in every thing you do."

Miss Anderson, on a crusade to make us all good mathematicians. Always superbly prepared, she made algebra music for us: "You can do it, and I expect you to do it."

And we did it, the entire class. She made the success of each of us the goal of all of us. Mrs. Anderson moved around that class with a passion that developed in each of us the consuming desire to excel at mathematics.

One vehicle that our teachers used to inculcate a sense of history, and a determination to make things better, was the "Devotions" period, held every day at fifteen minutes before noon. One teacher or the other would give an inspirational talk or read a great passage urging us to strive to do our best. Sometimes the program would open with the singing of a spiritual or of a patriotic song like "America, The Beautiful." Always we closed with a rousing rendition of "Lift Every Voice and Sing," written by James Weldon Johnson and popularly known as the Negro national anthem. It is a beautiful, melodious, passionate song, which invariably stirs deep feelings among black Americans.

Lift every voice and sing,
Till earth and heaven ring,
Ring with the harmonies of liberty.
Let our rejoicing rise,
High as the listening skies,
Let it resound loud as the rolling sea.
Sing a song full of the faith
That the dark past has taught us.
Sing a song, full of the hope
That the present has brought us.
Facing the rising sun,
Of our new day begun,
Let us march on,
Till victory is won.

God of our weary years,
God of our silent tears,
Thou who has brought us thus far on our way.
Thou who has by thy might
Led us into the light,
Keep us forever in the path we pray.
Lest our feet stray from the places
Our God where we met thee.
Lest, our hearts drunk with the wine
Of the world, we forget thee.
Shadowed beneath thy hand,
May we forever stand,
True to our God!
True to our native land!

The characters and personalities of our great, committed teachers led us to develop comfort with our identity as black Americans. They placed the mission ever before us: nothing less than freedom and equality. In our daily contacts with them they made us feel as co-conspirators in the struggle to bring the walls of racial injustice and discrimination down.

CHAPTER 8

Fallen to Pieces

MY FAMILY FELL TO PIECES in the third year of our residence on Thirteenth Avenue. My mother and my stepfather could find no work. The three dollars I brought home weekly from the golf course as a caddy were a major contribution to the family's income. The remainder came from my sister Sylvia's earnings as a dentist's assistant, five dollars per week.

Mother went to Cuba to be with my brother Raúl, who sought to continue his fight against tuberculosis there. In Cuba, Raúl would receive the best care available at the time, in a modern sanitarium. The funds for the trips were provided by my uncle Rogelio, who had opened a struggling dry-cleaning shop just before the Crash of 1929.

My sister Sylvia went to live with our aunt Gloria and her children. I remained with my stepsister, Mary, and my stepfather, Luis, in the triplex on Thirteenth Avenue. A part of our family for several years, he had moved in while we still lived on Eighth Avenue. A passive man, always smoking cigars, he never tried to give us guidance or to discipline us. His most vigorous attempt to influence our behavior, Mary's and mine, came as a softly stated, "You ought not do that." He spent most of his time out of the house, probably at the club playing cards or dominoes.

We stayed in the top unit of a ramshackle triplex on Thirteen Avenue above Twenty-second Street. For three months Mary and I took care of each other. Her father, my stepfather, remains but a blurred memory of this period in our disorganized lives. I cannot remember that he cooked. He left us to our own devices. Mary spent long periods away from the house, but she was always home before dark. We subsisted on rice, beans, biscuits, and oranges, which were always plentiful and inexpensive.

The eastern presence of the black American ghetto began at Twenty-second Street. Few black Cubans lived above Twenty-second Street. We then lived in a neighborhood where black Americans were in the majority by far, a

47

new experience for us. I enjoyed it thoroughly, for at my door was a play group which included me in all of its activities, especially in the exciting talks about sex in the early evenings.

We pooled our ignorance—which, I realized later, abounded.

"Girls can't get pregnant when they have the rag on," stated James, the oldest, most experienced, and most sophisticated of the group.

"Any of you guys ever had any?" he challenged.

"No, but I've felt some," answered Adrian truthfully, "and I've felt some nice boobs, too."

"Once, I had Roberta in the bushes, and I had her drawers almost off, but she panicked and ran," volunteered Johnny.

I sat silent, because I had not had much experience, mostly kissing and light petting through the girl's clothes. But the talks gave me the courage to try sex play with Cissie and Bunny, two girls on the periphery of the group.

The very next day we had a very exciting session at Cissie's house, which Cissie had to herself while her mother was at work. We three stripped down to our undergarments. The girls were in their slips. There was a lively discussion between Cissie and Bunny as to who would be first. Finally, Cissie volunteered.

I began to fondle her breasts through her slip. Small of breast, she did not wear a bra. This was my first experience with direct, intimate contact with a girl who had taken off her outer clothing. I felt very awkward, but excruciatingly excited, so much so that I trembled. Cissie was a pretty girl, and very spirited. She was the rough-and-tumble type, great fun to play with. She would wrestle with me, yet give no hint that she was trying to arouse me. I was her friend, that's all. Fortunately or unfortunately, she suddenly called a halt.

I think she knew what she was doing. The only opportunity I had for "heavy romance" in Tampa quickly came to an end, to my vast relief, for guilt pressed heavily upon my conscience. The wretchedness made the experience, in retrospect, confusing. I was excited, depressed, and frankly, pleased that I had enjoyed a certain intimacy with a girl. It seemed like some major and significant rite of passage had taken place. I was no longer one of the boys who had not even asked a girl. Cissie may have done us both good.

Nonetheless, I would travel a long road before I became comfortable making love to a woman. It was not until I was properly married, as the Church had dictated, that I was able to give myself fully to the sexual embrace.

Two very friendly families lived in the apartments below the unit my family occupied. Eva was two years older than I was, but, never mind, I fell in love with her. She enjoyed the attention, giving me little hugs and pinches, and displaying her ample, lovely cleavage to me often, while feigning that she was not aware that she was flirting with me. My flirtations with Eva stand out as one of the most enjoyable experiences of my early adolescent years.

I do not know how I escaped sex play with my stepsister Mary. We spent hours alone during the long summer days and nights. Mary was eighteen months older than I was, and in the fullness of her adolescent development. She walked around the house wearing nothing but panties and a thin nightgown. But she was my sister! It never occurred to me to try anything sinful with her, even though she confided to me that she was having sex with a friend of ours. I remember gazing with excitement at her large, lightly clothed, bosom. Her breasts were large and firm, and but loosely hidden under the diaphanous nightgown she sometimes wore. I enjoyed the views I had of their shape, form, and color. Yet in the three months we lived alone and together I don't remember ever seeing her uncovered breasts. I remember moments when I believed she was deliberately enticing me, but that was simple humanity, for neither of us would have touched the other, I believe.

My play group, the first one to which I belonged integrally, also saw to it that I learned how to swim. They taught me as they all had learned. They simply caught me by surprise and threw me into the river, under a bridge where I could find timbers to grasp if I got into trouble. Humberto and James kept a steady watch in the event that I should need help. I was terrified, but I had but one option: swim. Soon, I was taking the seven or eight strokes that would take me to one side of the bridge or the other.

The feelings of pride and exhilaration as I walked back to the neighborhood with my friends praising and congratulating me, made for a tremendous shift in my concept of myself. I belonged fully to the fraternity of boys now. The simple acts of feeling a girl's breasts and of learning how to swim had transformed me into an infinitely more confident boy. These rites of passage are always in my mind. I remember them clearly, vividly, and with deep feelings.

We received some kind of "relief," one of the programs which the new president, Franklin D. Roosevelt, initiated. A social worker came by weekly and made out vouchers, which we exchanged for clothes, flour, and butter at some facility in downtown Tampa.

The clothes were black, thick, hot woolen knickers, and shirts made of coarse blue denim material. Glad to get them, I wore them with no sense of diminished pride, for many of the boys wore them also. The flour, unleavened, came in twenty-five pound sacks. Two pounds of butter were issued with the flour. I walked all the way to downtown Tampa, and all the way back, about thirty-five blocks each way, to get the flour and butter. The fare for the trolley was five cents each way, an utterly unaffordable sum.

With the unleavened flour Mary and I made biscuits as well as we knew how. We had to eat them as soon as they were baked, for they became as hard as rocks upon cooling. Mary and I did what was most appropriate with the biscuits we did not eat: We played with them, throwing them at each other with yells of glee and delight.

I had just completed the tenth grade at Booker T. Washington High School, and I had not done very well. I received a D in Latin and a disgraceful C in English. Clearly on a downhill slide, I even cut classes and hung out in the home of a schoolmate who lived close to the campus and whose mother was not at home during the day.

I learned later that my teachers were very concerned about my downward slide. They apparently communicated their concern to Mr. Martin, who they knew had befriended me. They knew that *he* would be distressed.

CHAPTER 9

Going Up North

"BOY, WHEN ARE YOU GOING UP NORTH to get an education?" Mr. Martin had been after me all spring with the oft-repeated question. I didn't have the vaguest notion of how one went "up north."

Ultimately, during one of our Saturday morning trips to do his grocery shopping in the big markets downtown, where mostly white and mostly rich people shopped, he turned to me and said, "Boy, tell your momma to pack your clothes and give you five dollars. I'm taking you up north so you can get an education. Tell your momma to bring you to the insurance company at nine o'clock Wednesday morning ready to travel. You are going to Washington where you belong!"

Mr. Martin was the controller of the Central Life Insurance Company, a successful black-owned firm that served blacks in Florida. Very fair of skin, tall, thin, and lanky, he towered over black Tampa, determined to point every black adolescent possible towards college.

He did not cajole, exhort, or give too much advice. He simply made friends of us, so that we would have a first-hand experience of someone for whom college was a given, and who thought it was a given for us. He was especially helpful to us children of black Cuban immigrants, whose life experience did not include college as a vision of the possible.

The early generation of black Cubans, including my mother, had come in waves of migration to the United States. Most were, on the whole, literate. Some were very well read. But I do not know of any that attended college.

Had it not been for Mr. Martin and our black American teachers, it would have been very difficult for us to land places in black American life and, however limited, in the American society. They shoe-horned us in, the very few lucky ones among us.

We gathered in front of the insurance company at nine o'clock, as Mr. Martin had told me. My mother, my uncle Rojelio, my sister Sylvia, and I all joined Mr. Martin, Mr. G.D. Rogers, the president of the insurance company, and his son, G.D. Rogers, Jr. We transferred the paper shopping bag that held my clothes to Mr. Roger's car.

"Hi, Evelio, we're ready," greeted the ebullient Mr. Martin. He moved easily among his small crew of employees, which had gathered to wish us goodbye. He exchanged greetings with my mother.

"Now don't you worry, Mrs. Grillo, this is the best thing for Evelio. He'll be all right," Mr. Martin consoled my sad-faced mother. Letting me go took all of her emotional strength.

She had pawned her engagement ring for five dollars. She would redeem it for seven dollars and fifty cents two weeks later.

I thought I caught a certain wistfulness in my sister's face and voice. Four years older than I, Sylvia had watched each of the older boys leave Tampa seeking opportunity. Now I, younger than she, had my opportunity. Why did she always have to stay behind?

"We'll have to hurry along," remarked Mr. Martin, eager to begin the trip. It was a long way to Jacksonville, the first stop. So the leave takings were brief, almost abrupt, while yet noisily happy.

The scene became a blur as we pulled away, Mr. Rogers and Junior in the front seat, and Mr. Martin and I in the rear. My mother's face, its severity softened by sadness, was but background to the chatter of leave taking. I had neither the time nor the inclination to give her the attention she sought from me. I was going up north!

Jacksonville lay two hundred miles away, a long trip by 1934 standards. After we left Tampa and were well on the road, things began to unfold for me. Mr. Martin and Mr. Rogers were going to Richmond, Virginia, to attend an insurance convention. Mr. Rogers had brought his son along for a vacation. At seventeen, Junior was two years older than I, so he could help with the driving. Mr. Martin, I surmised, had been planning for some time to take me along.

Mr. Martin and Mr. Rogers were in their late forties or early fifties. Mr. Rogers, a civil and gentle man, engaged me in brief conversation about my hopes and plans. G.D. Junior felt that he was much older than I was, and rightfully so. More experienced than I was by quantums, he clearly took charge when he and I were alone together.

I was subdued and quiet during the drive to Jacksonville. At one point, I gave Mr. Martin the five dollars my mother had procured. Mr. Martin took it quietly and, without drawing the attention of Mr. Rogers and Junior, placed it in an envelope and then placed the envelope in his inside jacket pocket.

The last time I remember thinking of my mother throughout the trip and in the months ahead in Washington, the years of fearing her had ended. Without being even vaguely aware of what was transpiring, I was pushing her deep into the recesses of my spirit. While relatively quiet, within I boiled with self-centered excitement. I had not even said goodbye to my sister or to my uncle.

We arrived in Jacksonville while yet enough light remained for us to make the complicated arrangements for lodging, which the times imposed. We went to a local funeral parlor where blacks could be guided to a local home that rented rooms to black travelers. The motels and hotels were off limits, restricted to whites only. Mr. Martin and Mr. Rogers went into the funeral parlor, leaving G.D. Junior and me in the car.

When they returned, they had connected to the home. We drove there. When Mr. Martin and Mr. Rogers had arranged for their lodging, G.D. Junior drove the two of us back to the funeral parlor.

We parked under a street light in front of the mortuary and settled in for the night, stopped in what seemed to be the commercial section within the black ghetto. Junior and I slept in the car the entire night without the slightest interruption. We were sojourners escaping to the north, and we were not to be bothered. The police and kindly adults saw to that.

We awakened with the first streak of light. G. D. Junior, pleased with the responsibility given him, drove us back to the house where his father and Mr. Martin had spent the night.

I don't remember where—or if—G.D. Junior and I washed our hands and faces. Mr. Rogers and Mr. Martin were waiting for us; bags packed and ready to be placed again in the car. We drove back to the commercial district.

Dawn had yielded to bright, sparkling day. We went to a good-sized restaurant for breakfast. Mr. Martin led the way in. He did not rush, but he smoothed his imposing frame past the door and called out to the waiter in a folksy, raspy, drawl: "Hi there! I hear you cook up some fine grits here, and I hear that your biscuits aren't bad at all."

His presence filled the room. His simple, open, manner quickly caught the attention of the waiter, who bustled towards him, all smiles. While the waiter was showing us to our table, Mr. Martin kept up a continuous banter about the proper way to cook grits, and the proper way to make biscuits. He waited for us to be seated, but he did not sit down. Instead, he walked to the kitchen, the waiter at his side, chattering that he wanted to talk it over with the cook and that, after all, he hailed from Tampa, where grits and biscuits were cooked to perfection. He disappeared into the kitchen. Shortly, we could hear voices in mock dispute over the relative merits of Jacksonville and Tampa grits and biscuits. He emerged a few minutes later with the entire kitchen staff in tow, smiling and talking animatedly. His voice carried throughout the restaurant.

"Come with me. I have someone I want you to meet." This was vintage Mr. Martin, and I was enjoying him thoroughly. He led the procession of four staff members, dressed in kitchen whites, until they formed a semi-circle around the table where Mr. Rogers, G. D. Junior, and I were seated. Then he said, his eyes ablaze with delight, "Meet my friend Evelio. He's going up north to get an education."

A happy buzz of chatter followed as they each shook my hand warmly, gleefully commenting about my going to college, asking me what I intended to be, and, generally, making a happy fuss over an absolutely splendid young man, a future leader, no less!

The center of a warm circle of love and encouragement, I felt special and very important to those surrounding me. It was not until this ceremony of indoctrination had played its full course that we ordered our grits and biscuits.

Mr. Martin and Mr. Rogers kept up a steady stream of commentary about the countryside as we made our way through the cotton and tobacco fields of Georgia, South Carolina, and North Carolina. They loved the land, yet hated it, too, for they were under constant assault because they were black.

We had an accident between Fayetteville and Raeford. G. D. Junior drove this long stretch of lonely, narrow concrete, recently built. Red dirt, through which the dozers had but recently gashed, lay on either side of the highway. A heavy rain-washed mud lay across the road.

G.D. Junior, all seventeen years of him, drove downhill into this invitation to disaster. He drove without having the knowledge of how to gear the car down from freewheeling. The car spun all the way around, rolled over and then landed, almost gently, on its side in the soft mud.

We survived the crash. The only injury was to Mr. Roger's arm, and that was not very serious. Every second of the experience as the car was spinning and rolling over is recorded in my memory, like a sequence from a slow-motion film. As we were speeding down the hill, Mr. Martin started giving Junior warnings about road conditions and the speed of the car. But Junior did not know how to control the car or even how to reduce its speed. As the car went into a spin near the bottom of the hill, Mr. Martin cried out, "See there! See there! Oh! Oh! We're going to Hell!"

Mr. Rogers softer voice pleaded with Junior to exercise caution, and, as we went into the spin, he cried out softly, "Oh! My goodness!" He was a gentleman even in this moment of fear and great crisis.

During the infinite seconds between the beginning of the spin and the landing of the car in the mud, we were rigid and steeled for the calamity. Frozen in time and space, not a sound came from any of us.

As soon as the car finished its hurtle, pandemonium descended. Mr. Rogers called out frantically for Junior, and Mr. Martin called out, "Evelio! Evelio! Are you all right?"

I answered quickly, "I'm all right, Mr. Martin, I'm all right!"

Junior was simultaneously giving Mr. Rogers the same assurances. A moment of quiet settled over the disordered scene, as we realized that our worst fears had not come to pass.

We extricated ourselves from the morass, slowly. Mr. Rogers and Mr. Martin were all over Junior and me, assuring themselves that we were not hurt. Mr. Martin's affection and concern showed demonstrably in his face and in his eyes as he checked to see that I was, indeed, unharmed. This interlude with Mr. Martin I savored as a fathering moment, though I could not have expressed it that way at the time. I basked in the radiance of his love, his care, and his concern. I had not been that close to a man since my father's death, eleven years previously. This was a very rare and special moment. My father had died when I was three. I do not remember his face. But I remember his presence and his love, as when he was talking gently to me as he handed me some new trinket. Mr. Martin's tenderness stirred in me a surge of great affection for him, similar to the feelings I remember having for my father.

A white farmer came running in a few moments and helped us to gather our disheveled selves together. A police auto shortly followed and, some time thereafter, a tow truck. They towed us into Fayettesville, where arrangements to make the car operable were made.

The awkward arrangements to find lodging for the night were completed also, but I do not remember them. My memory kicks in the next morning, when we were having breakfast, before we took off for Richmond, the last leg of our journey together.

Mr. Martin again brought out the kitchen staff to meet me and to offer words of congratulations and encouragement. By this time the cultural indoctrination was taking. I began to feel the purpose of going to college forming within me. For the first time in my life I began to see myself in a college setting.

We arrived in Richmond in the very late afternoon. Mr. Rogers and Junior left Mr. Martin and me at the house of Mr. Martin's uncle, where Mr. Martin was staying during the convention, and where I was to spend the night.

The uncle, Mr. Brown, was a gray-headed delight. He was retired post-office clerk (a very prestigious position for a black American at that time), and his house was the most luxurious I had ever slept in. In the perspective of time, though, I now believe it to have been simply a solid, well-kept home in what was then a middle-class black neighborhood.

Mr. Martin and Mr. Brown turned their attention to my continued acculturation. In the early evening, Mr. Martin took me into the black commercial district, which excited me almost unbearably.

We walked past the main theater, where the marquee screamed in foot-high letters against a dazzling white lighted background that BUTTERBEANS AND SUSIE were playing in person. Mr. Martin, aware of my excitement and of the absolute strangeness of the experience for me, explained that Butterbeans and Susie were a very popular comedy act. We walked down the street taking in all that there was to see. It was all new, very bright, and very beautiful. I had never been close to a big extravagantly lighted marquee before. This was my first experience with the bright lights of a big city. Not even New York City generated the excitement of my evening in Richmond.

We stopped at a restaurant. Mr. Martin, impelled by the desire to provide new experiences for me, suggested that I have a club sandwich. He must have known that I had never had one before. In fact, I never had eaten in a restaurant before this trip. Nor had I ever eaten turkey.

The club sandwich was a transforming experience. I gazed with fascination at the layers of turkey, ham, and strips of bacon, the slices of tomato, and the garnish of lettuce. Even the mayonnaise was a new taste for me. In my home, a sandwich had been, invariably, a slice of bologna between two slices of white bread lightly splashed with mustard, nothing else. Three slices of bread contained this sandwich. More than one sandwich, as I knew sandwiches. I took my time eating this new, huge, delicious concoction, savoring every mouthful.

Mr. Martin watched me with obvious great pleasure at my enjoyment of what was clearly a totally new cultural experience for me. He urged me to have a slice of pie and a glass of milk to finish the meal.

We walked home slowly. I was happy, excited, tired, and a little sobered by the realization that this was my last evening with Mr. Martin. I did not understand what he had done for me, but I felt it viscerally. He had given me himself. My excitement was not so much about the trip, the places we had seen, the people we had met. I was moved by very deep feelings. I had been very close to an older, loving, man for three whole days, an experience unique in my childhood after my father's death.

The next morning at six o'clock, Mr. Martin's uncle came to the room in which I slept. I was awaiting him eagerly. He had asked me to take a walk along the St. Charles River with him. The river could not have been far from the house, for I do not remember walking a long distance. We started along its grassy shore, all the while Mr. Martin's uncle pointing out one interesting sight or the other. Then, as though he had known me all my life, he began to talk gently and seriously to me.

"You have made me a very happy man," he began. "Ever since Mr. Martin told me that you were going up north to go to school, I have been feeling good. I know you are a good student, because you have a fine mind and a very pleasant disposition. I just had to say that to you because what you are about to do is important for all of us."

I did not quite understand everything he said to me but I did grasp the tenor and the emotion of it. Without planning it, he had participated in the process whereby college came for the first time to loom as a possibility for me.

That's what Mr. Martin's goal had been during the journey from Tampa to Richmond. That had been his goal when he first hired me to chase balls on the tennis court where he and Dr. Ervin, Mr. Broughton, and others of the black middle class played.

Mr. Martin provided the final episode in what I now understand clearly as an acculturation process. They led me deliberately and lovingly into the assumption that college was a matter-of-fact choice for me. By the end of the trip, attending college became a given. The only thing remaining to be worked out was how I would pull it off.

Mr. Martin was his most engaging self as he drove me to the bus station, where I was to take a bus to Washington, D.C. He kept up a steady chatter, letting me know that he was going to miss me and talking about the wonders of Washington.

We arrived at the bus station. Mr. Martin purchased a ticket and handed it to me. Then he walked with me to the bus. Then, just before I boarded, he reached into his inside jacket pocket, brought out an envelope, took out the very same five-dollar bill my mother had given me, and that I had in turn given to him, and gave it back to me. His last words, imprinted indelibly in my memory, were: "Son, now you go up there and show them what a *southern* colored boy can do."

CHAPTER 10

Washington, D.C.

MY ARRIVAL IN WASHINGTON all but paralyzed my brother, Henry. What could he do with me? He acted as though he wanted to hug me with joy even while he despaired of the responsibility that had suddenly fallen upon him. Henry was a very serious type, very focused on whatever task was at hand. Now I became his task. He had to make many arrangements. Reality soon asserted its energizing force, and he began to plan.

"You'll have to sleep on the floor," he said, thinking out loud. "I'll have to inform my landlady that you've joined me, so that she can adjust the rent. I'll have to find a larger, more adequate room. You'll have to find a job, any job, quicker than now."

At any rate, I slept on the floor, was delivering newspapers within three days, and had begun as a caddy at Chevy Chase Country Club by the second Saturday afternoon. As a caddy, I made one dollar and ten cents per round. I could caddy one round on Saturday afternoon, two rounds on Sunday, and one round on Wednesday afternoons, since it was summer and schools were closed.

So I earned as much as four dollars a week, after I subtracted the trolley fare. Good money for a fifteen-year-old at that time. My brother welcomed it as a contribution to our support.

Caddying loomed large as part of my adolescence. The Caddy Master assigned the bags to us in the order in which we had signed up. So, to be sure of getting a bag to carry, many of us arrived at the golf course on the first street car, at 6 AM. Then we waited until noon, when the golfers began arriving.

Those six hours we spent fighting boredom, playing cards, spinning yarns, reading newspapers and old magazines, doing what we could do to deal with the oppressive heat and the humidity. Petty gambling occupied the time of many. An occasional fight, some quite bloody, served to teach us smaller and younger boys to stay out of the way.

58

Some older men, victims of the Depression, displayed their knowledge and verbal skills in conversations among them, discussing literature and history, and even reciting simple poetry. I learned a lot in the bull pen, the open enclosure within which we passed the long hours until a bag was assigned to us. Mercifully, a few large trees sheltered us from the blazing sun. When the rains fell, we packed into a small room, hot, sweaty, and very stuffy.

In time, I began to deliver prescriptions and sundries for a pharmacy three evenings a week. Earlier, I had found work as a vendor at Griffith Stadium, where the Washington Senators played major-league baseball, and where the Washington Redskins played professional football in the National Football League. The job as a vendor was quite lucrative for the times. I could make from one to three four dollars whenever there was an event at the stadium.

On the day Joe DiMaggio broke the record for hitting in consecutive games, I made twenty-one dollars, all "from the muscle," or honestly. (There were several ways by which vendors could steal from the concessionaire.) A double header (two games) had filled the stadium to capacity, and the heat and humidity baked and stultified the fans. All food and drinks were sold by the end of the first game. So, I scrubbed out a bucket we used to carry bottled soft drinks, filled it with ice and water, and gave the water away, not unmindful that many recipients would want to tip me.

And tip me they did! Quarters and half dollars! It was the largest amount of money I had ever made in a single day. I gave it all to my brother, to help pay for my keep. He seemed relieved that I contributed substantially to defraying the expenses that I generated.

Though still making only a modest income, I paid my way fully, and I contributed to the sum that Henry sent mother weekly to help her in Tampa. I considered myself very lucky, for the Great Depression had descended in full force and yet I had work.

The Depression was evident in the breadlines, the lines of hundreds of applicants for a few jobs, the homelessness, the shabby clothes worn by many people, the manufacturing and commerce operating at the slowest possible pace (or not at all), the suicides over lost fortunes. The Great Depression led to a general sense of psychic depression in the entire populace.

My own good luck might never have materialized without Henry, who, despite a difficult temper, took good care of me and carried out dutifully his function as my guardian. He was my own special safety net while he worked as a bookbinder in the schools, a government-subsidized position.

We moved up the Georgia Avenue Hill to Gresham Place from Florida Avenue, where I had first landed. I have nothing but wonderful feelings about this period of my life, my last two years in high school. For the first time in my life, I did not have to walk the black Cuban/black American cultural tightrope that summer.

Only a sprinkling of black Cubans who identified with black Americans lived in Washington at the time. They spoke English well. Those who spoke little or no English lived in the Latin ghetto which was then forming. We lived in a black American neighborhood near the Howard University campus. Considered simply a black boy, I had the freedom to move about the ghetto and to enjoy the marvels that blacks could enjoy in Washington. Only newcomers like me could appreciate the richness of black Washington life and culture then.

The intersection of "U" Street (the commercial artery of the black ghetto) and Fourteenth Street formed the heart of the ghetto. Crowded with traffic, it bustled with the noises of small businesses. The three motion-picture theaters—the Republic, the Lincoln, and the Booker T.—enjoyed booming crowds. The Howard Theater offered live acts of the caliber of Duke Ellington and the great comic Pigmeat Markham.

Saturday afternoon was date time. The Republic and the Lincoln were always crowded with children of the middle class. Many seemed paired up for their weekly session of lovemaking. I missed much of this fun, since I usually worked on Saturdays. But occasionally I slipped in a session with a lovely sophomore or junior, and found the arrangement and atmosphere very conducive to kissing and smooching.

Howard University, "proudly there on hilltop high," gave center and focus to the entire black middle class. Georgia Avenue served as the spine which carried one up the hill to Howard University and beyond. Along its flanks lived a good segment of Washington's black lower-middle and upper-lower classes, with a goodly number of upper middle-class families sprinkled among them. Many landlords and landladies made their livings by providing room and board to Howard students.

Though segregation thrived in Washington, the federal presence made it much less strident than that which I had known in Tampa. We were free to sit anywhere on public transportation. That difference alone made Washington a wonderland for me. We did not have to go to the backs of busses and trolleys. We had access to many facilities, except schools, operated by the District of Columbia government. Although facilities were operated discriminatorily as to employment and management, everyone generally had access to services. This included the libraries, which were both a great resource and a great source of pleasure to me.

We had the numerous and various resources of the federal government open to us, although we did not have anything approaching equal opportunity in employment. Commercial places of public accommodation, such as theaters and restaurants, were still closed to blacks. It was still clear that we occupied a second-class status. While we could rub shoulders with whites, we did not have access to the world of opportunities open to them. But we could enjoy federal governmental venues, places like the National Archives, the awe-inspiring Library of Congress, and the Lincoln Memorial, among many others. Non-governmental or quasi-governmental institutions added to the rich panoply of places to enjoy. The exquisite National Gallery of Art and the various settings of the Smithsonian Institution brought me great pleasure.

Among the most spectacular events I could attend were the Watergate Concerts presented by the National Symphony Orchestra. I did not know much about classical music, and I had never seen or heard an orchestra in person. Bill Daley, a young man who took a liking to me, introduced me to this wonderland of great music. Moonlight, water, the Lincoln Memorial lighted so gracefully, the reflecting pool capturing bits of the scene, the endless expanses of freshly mown grass, and the balmy Washington summer nights, all wrapped us in surges of joy. Thrills coursed through me in ceaseless waves as all of my senses absorbed the beauty of so many combined, harmonious elements. I never saw Bill Daley again after I finished high school, but I have never forgotten him or his sensitivity.

Washington also had a Recreation and Parks Department which provided large fields of green in which to run, modern pools in which to swim, courts on which to play. None of these were available to blacks in Tampa, so the contrast made a tremendous impression upon me. There was still much discrimination against blacks. That loomed as the ugly side of Washington, an ugliness with which I became very familiar. But for one who had spent the first fifteen years of life in the ghetto in dismal Tampa, Washington was every bit a fairyland!

No matter what fetters others felt, I was free: free to ride the bus and sit anywhere, free to go to the library and caress those marvelous books, free to enjoy so many things I could not even dream of in Tampa. Most of all, and this I know only by hindsight, I was free to be unambiguously black.

CHAPTER 11

Dunbar High

IN AUGUST, NEWSPAPERS carried a notice advising all newcomers of school age to come to the school of their choice to be enrolled and classified. Henry and I went to Dunbar High School on the appointed day. We had a conference with a Mr. Shippen, a nervous man who nonetheless had penetrating, kind eyes.

Mr. Shippen seemed puzzled as he reviewed my transcript.

"We have found," he began, "that students who transfer in from the South tend to be more successful if they repeat their last year. This allows them to adjust to the pace here at Dunbar."

Henry began to get agitated and I quietly kicked him, to keep him out of the discussion, for I had information that he didn't have. I had been looking over the desk at the upside-down transcript that had come from Booker Washington High School. It had been radically altered to insure my placement in the college-track program. There was no entry for wood shop, for example. I had two years of wood shop in Tampa. I had had only one year of Latin, and I had done poor work in the subject. The transcript gave me credit for two full years of Latin. I also had credit for a year of history that I never took. Moreover, the transcript showed mostly A's, with an occasional B sprinkled here and there. The conspiracy to point me towards college apparently had been joined by our principal in Tampa, Mr. S. H. Newsome.

Mr. Shippen waited for my response to his suggestion about repeating the tenth grade. I remained silent, but I am certain that I had a crestfallen look upon my face. Mr. Shippen took another puzzled look at my transcript. Then he spoke again.

"How would you like to try the eleventh grade for six weeks. If you find that the work is too hard for you, we'll go back to the tenth grade, but at least you will have tried."

Containing my glee was difficult. I restrained myself and said, "I will be grateful for the opportunity and I will study very hard."

Mr. Shippen then closed with, "All right, why don't we try it?"
We shook hands all around, and Henry and I left.

I had the lightest, most pleasant interlude with Henry during the walk back home after the interview. Henry was a stern person, compulsively focused on work and occupied otherwise with his girl friends. There never was much banter between us. But the successful encounter with Mr. Shippen softened him.

"I am very proud of you. We showed him that to be from the South is not necessarily a sign of backwardness. You handled that very well, I thought."

He put his arm around my shoulder by way of demonstrating his affection. I appreciated this gesture, for I had been unsure of Henry's commitment to me, given the surprise of my arrival on his doorstep. This experience seemed to strengthen his determination to care for me. My feelings, reciprocally, warmed to him.

Dunbar exceeded all of my expectations as a school! It had such an uncommon, distinguished faculty. To me, it was simply another of Washington's marvels. It had three physics laboratories, three chemistry laboratories, and three biology laboratories, a very large and commodious library, tennis courts, the largest swimming pool I had ever seen, a cavernous armory where we were to drill in our dashing military uniforms, and a very large auditorium with the words of Paul Laurence Dunbar painted on the walls in foot-high script:

KEEP A PLUGGIN' AWAY!
KEEP A PLUGGIN' AWAY!
PERSEVERANCE STILL IS KING!
LIFE ITS SURE REWARD WILL BRING!
KEEP A PLUGGIN' AWAY!

I took Paul Laurence Dunbar at his word. I memorized my geometry theorems and I did all of my homework before I went to sleep at night. Interestingly enough, I had a difficult time with Spanish, because Mrs. Daly insisted that I place the accents in their proper places. For all of my fluency in Spanish, I did not know anything about accents. At any rate, there was no mention of returning to the tenth grade when the six-weeks trial came to an end.

At that time, three high schools were provided for blacks in Washington. Whatever their history, the schools clearly reflected a separation of students by social classes. Armstrong High, right across the street from Dunbar, offered vocational educational. Cardoza High School, about ten blocks away, served those who were preparing for work in the business world, largely as secretaries and bookkeepers. Dunbar served an educational elite. It dedicated itself entirely to the preparation of students for college. Students came to the schools from the black community as a whole.

Named for the celebrated black poet Paul Laurence Dunbar, the school drew its students from the large Washington black upper, middle, and upper-lower economic classes. Children of employees of the federal government, I believe, constituted a large segment of the student body. The parents of many held government jobs as elevator operators, janitors, messengers, clerical personnel, and, perhaps, some administrative personnel. Nonetheless, they earned high salaries when compared to Washington's black population as a whole. Moreover, their jobs remained relatively secure during the Great Depression. They were then, as they are now, the basis of Washington's relatively large black middle class. The children of persons employed in service capacities constituted another substantial group of students. Their parents worked in the retail business establishments. Others worked in the homes of affluent families. Children of faculty members of Howard University, Miner Teachers College, of teachers in the public schools, children of professionals, of small business owners, of lawyers, of doctors, of dentists, of accountants, of ministers, of nurses, and the like, all set the tone of the school.

Dunbar was their college-prep school. It competed successfully for a place in the academic firmament with the private prep schools of New England. Only a very few families could afford to send their children to the prestigious private prep schools of the Northeast. Dunbar was their school of choice because it provided a great education, under brilliant teachers, in an atmosphere that breathed serious, hard study.

Behaviorally attractive because the standards were set by the middle- and upper-class students, and by an upper-class faculty, Dunbar was the place to be socially, so great was its prestige. Aspiring families who lived in neighboring Virginia and Maryland communities found ways of enrolling their children at Dunbar.

There was ample room and quiet assistance, such as free lunches, for those children who did not have much money. I was one of these, though I lost my status as underprivileged when Henry secured a position as a clerk in a federal government agency at the then-magnificent salary of ninety dollars per month, or $1,080 per year.

Dunbar's great faculty, drawn from the rich pool of black educators who were effectively locked out of teaching opportunities in white colleges and secondary schools, set very high standards for themselves and for their students. College was the assumed goal of all Dunbar students. I don't remember a single classmate who did not attend college somewhere. Most of them went to Howard University or to Miner Teachers College. Many attended Ivy League schools in New England.

An institution of about three thousand students, Howard was known as "The Capstone of Negro Education." The most prestigious college to which black educators could aspire for academic posts at the time, it offered a faculty of nationally and internationally recognized scholars. Howard not only provided excellent undergraduate instruction, but also great graduate programs including outstanding schools and colleges of law, dentistry, medicine, music, art, and graduate programs in the humanities and sciences.

A large number of the teachers and administrators who staffed Washington's segregated black schools pursued their education at Miner Teacher's College. A public institution, Miner was supported by property taxes and by the annual grant by the U.S. Congress to the city of Washington. No tuition was charged at Miner. An excellent college education was available even to those who had little money. Many students who attended Miner did not become teachers. Some of Dunbar's most outstanding students, those committed to education as a career, chose Miner as their college.

I was assigned to Boys' Section "A" homeroom. Among my fellow members of the section were the nephew of an assistant superintendent of schools, the son of world-renowned scientist Ernest Everett Just, the son of two teachers in the school system who were married to each other, the son of a prominent local physician, the son of a highly successful local photographer, the son of a very prominent minister, and the sons of middle-rank federal government officials. Fully half of the members of Section "A" were children of prominent professionals in the community.

My classes were a delight: English, geometry, Spanish, chemistry, history, and physical education, wherein I played organized baseball for the first time in my life. As I remember, we had no physical education instruction in Tampa.

The quality of our weekly assemblies exceeded by far that of anything I had ever experienced. Our school could call on superb black speakers from Howard University and from the federal government. Excellent scholars addressed us.

I remember most vividly the renowned historian Dr. Charles Wesley, an author, college president, and great preacher, who spoke to us two or three times. In ringing oratory, he would lift our spirits with discussions of the black historical past. He would inspire us with hope and faith in our future in a more just society, which surely would come. The assemblies confirmed us as future leaders, generating fervor and determination.

We also heard recitals by excellent black artists on the rise. We enjoyed particularly our own fellow student George Walker, who was considered a prodigy. His favorite composition was Nathaniel Dett's "Juba Dance," a dramatic piece with an African motif, which George played with great force and power, making a sound that overwhelmed us and left us thrilled and limp with excitement. He recently won a Pulitzer Prize in composition.

Into this rarified atmosphere I was dropped. Clearly a bumpkin from the South, I was looked down upon because of my dress and my awkward, anxious demeanor. Besides, I spoke Spanish, and that, too, made me a strange one. I differed from the other students with foreign backgrounds, such as the children of diplomats from the Caribbean families. I felt more at home in the black American milieu than they did. My acculturation by the black American community of Tampa had taken. I *thought* black American. I *felt* black American. So, generally, my classmates took me in as just another black boy. There was still an uneasiness about me, but I attribute that to the differences in economic status between my classmates and me, and my blunders in verbal expressions foreign to them.

I think, too, that I tensed up in groups of boys. My mother's rigid prohibition of any play in boys" groups must have led to a certain social incompetence on my part. I believe that I compensated for my insecurity by competitive, even conceited, academic functioning.

Some of my classmates became warm friends, something like my experience in Tampa, I was invited by two classmates to visit in their homes, even though I could not reciprocate because my brother and I lived in a single room, in a rooming house without kitchen privileges. We ate our evening meal at a boarding house about three blocks from our home, and we scrounged for breakfast and lunch.

Only one classmate kept me off balance by drawing attention to gross language miscues and inappropriate behavior on my part. In retrospect, I believe he was threatened by my challenge to his position as one of the top students in the class.

One incident was dramatic—and traumatic for me. Jim and I met in a small group chatting in the hall. I don't remember what we were talking about, but in the midst of much laughter, I blurted out "You Negroes!" in a mock-deprecating manner. Coming from anyone else in the group, this would have been understood as the charade, played out almost daily by black people, of imitating white people exclaiming in exasperation about black behv ior. It is very common in-group humor among blacks.

After the group dissolved, each member going to his particular class, Jim must have organized the lynching party, drawing attention to my words as an indication that I really did not consider myself black. Mrs. Brown, our home-room teacher, apparently became aware that something was amiss. As I learned later, she spoke to one of the boys who told her what had happened. She quickly convened the members of the group who witnessed my *faux pas*. Having had no idea of anything unusual going on, the meeting caught me by surprise and unprepared.

Mrs. Brown introduced the subject, stating that she had become aware of a serious situation that she believed needed airing. To my complete surprise, Jim began recounting the incident and raising the question regarding my identity as a black. His face distorted with contempt for me, he had his nose tilted upward as though he were smelling something awful. No one else made any remarks. I believe that the other boys sympathized with my plight as Jim's victim.

Outraged, I attempted a few words of protest and defense, but I succeeded only in fuming. Finally, I began to sob quietly and disconsolately, feeling utterly defeated. My reaction must have sobered the group, for no one spoke for a full minute or two.

Then Mrs. Brown spoke softly. "I could not believe that what I heard actually happened. I hope that the matter has been cleared up. I know that you won't permit yourselves to be so unkind again." Actually, the boys were not very contrite, for they really had not participated fully in the travesty. They simply were following Jim, one of the two or three top students in the class, and certainly one of the most powerful.

The son of a very prominent Baptist minister, he came from a prestigious family. I believe that he fancied himself the social arbiter of the group, protecting the purity of the in-group of children of professionals. The others were more like bystanders as Jim carried out the mischievous and successful effort to put me in my place.

I was an easy target, for I had the permanent status of newcomer and outsider. I had entered Dunbar in the eleventh grade, whereas the class had established its social pecking order one year previously, in the tenth grade, and perhaps even earlier, in the junior-high schools. Besides, my behavior did not endear me to my classmates. I talked much more than I listened, and, in the manner of the very insecure, I had strong opinions about matters about which I knew very little. Besides, I had no pedigree. Clearly, I was near the bottom of the pecking order in "A" section. In Tampa, I had been a black boy fairly well integrated into the group. This was not the case in school in Washington. I had to earn my spurs all over again.

Jim feigned regret, condescendingly, and said words implying that, now that he understood, he would permit me to remain in the circle of *bona fide* blacks. The other boys quickly reassured me, convinced now of my legitimacy.

I left the room, confused, angry, and crestfallen. I walked home from school that afternoon in a daze. I did not tell anyone what had happened, not even Henry. I do not know why I remained silent. Perhaps I could not talk about the incident without breaking up. That provided sufficient motive for silence. Moreover, I carried a certain guilt, for I believed I must have done something wrong, since I drew this much attention. I have resented Jim all of my life. Not even his death several years ago has softened the feeling.

An unmistakable color line operated at Dunbar. Brown-skinned and light-skinned students predominated in every aspect of school life except athletics. Few very black students stood out in the school population. Those that did were academically brilliant or very talented. Their academic achievement did not always provide enhanced social status.

There was and there remains great resentment of the differential treatment accorded the dark, especially the very dark, students. To this day, some classmates refuse to participate in alumni activities, still harboring the resentment they experienced as adolescents in a color-based value system wherein they were the least prized as members.

I was brown-skinned. I passed the brown paper bag test.

"If you're light, you're all right; if you're brown, stick around; if you're black, stay back" is one ditty that the very black persons heard resentfully.

I believe I carried less baggage with respect to color. In Tampa, very black students had not been as differentiated with respect to popularity and leadership roles as they were in Washington. Moreover, I was a black Cuban, a member of definite language and cultural minority. In Tampa I had become accustomed to accepting black Americans, including a large number of very dark ones, as role models for my behavior. Generally, I escaped the resentment of my Dunbar fellow students with respect to the color issue.

I navigated the Dunbar waters with relative success during my eighteen months there. My teachers were generous and kind to me. I believe that they felt a special warmth for me as an underdog, having no mother or father, and living socially and economically on the other side of the tracks.

That faculty was a very impressive group, an aristocracy manifesting great dignity, almost all of them earning the high respect and even awe of their students. Even those in declining in years and in abilities played well the role of aristocrat, meticulous in their dress and infallibly courteous to students. Most were graduates of prestigious universities. The majority of them held master's degrees. Some had earned doctorates. My schoolmates were also a very impressive group. Straight-A students abounded. Some had reputations that extended far beyond the school. Their families had produced generations of brilliant, accomplished graduates. A measure of the quality and talent of the Dunbar students can be found in a litany of names of graduates who achieved national renown. Edward Brooke, the most prominent, became the first black to serve in the U. S. Senate since Reconstruction.

I was helped to succeed at Dunbar by the sound education in English, speech, and dramatics that I had received at St. Peter Claver's. During my first year at Dunbar, I placed second to a polished, very bright, exceptional young woman, Victoria Todd, in the oratorical contest and, again, in the citywide contest which followed.

In my senior year, I won first place in the Dunbar High contest, rested on my laurels, and was soundly trounced in the city-wide contest by Evelyn Tymous, a classmate who had finished second to me in the Dunbar High contest. She won so convincingly that, though disappointed and embarrassed, I could not but agree with the decision. I have admired Evelyn greatly throughout the years.

I walked to and from school, whatever the weather. I don't remember a single automobile driven by any student to school. Some students may have been dropped off by family members, and many used public transportation. But the majority, like me, walked from the ghetto radiating from the intersections of East Capitol, West Capitol, North Capitol, and South Capitol Avenues. The Northwestern quadrant housed the major institutions of the black community: the three high schools, Howard University, Miner Teachers College, the four major theaters, the major churches, and the black business hub.

Dunbar offered also Army cadet training, my favorite activity. Fully half of the boys participated in this after-school activity. On drill days, we wore snappy uniforms, which the girls admired. Training was rigorous and very disciplined. We were taught the manual of arms with real rifles, and the intricate steps and formations involved in close order drill.

One day a year, the three high schools participated in an annual drill competition held at Griffith Stadium, the major-league baseball park. Dunbar invariably won this competition. The annual competition took stage during the week as the major event on the school and community's calendars. Practically all of the students, and most of families of participants, attended the spectacular pageant.

The combined complements from the three high schools formed the city's cadet brigade, commanded by a student colonel. The selection of the colonel, and of the lieutenant colonels of the individual schools, was thought by some to be somehow enmeshed in political maneuvering, but I was not close enough to the center of things to judge. From the perspective of the present, I believe that politics was a natural and expected component of the process.

We won awards in many categories: The most coveted was that for best company. The banner denoting this signal achievement flew along with the particular company's flag throughout the ensuing year. The members of the company strutted with understandable pride whenever they had an opportunity to display the prized banner.

The girls proudly wore armbands provided by their boyfriends, a tradition passed on from generation to generation. Highly coveted, the armbands carried with them the honor of allowing the cadet to sit with his chosen girl during the periods when he was not on the field competing. I managed to have my armband worn by a very pretty sophomore. She had waged a subtle and effective campaign to have me choose her without having it appear that she had chosen me.

Life was being very good during the spring of my senior year at Dunbar. I believe I would have received some prize at graduation had not events intervened. I had been elected president of the Student Council in an election clearly influenced by the vice-principal, Miss Brooks, to favor me. I worked daily and weekends at Griffith Stadium selling peanuts, and two evenings a week sold soft drinks at the local arena, which offered boxing and wrestling matches. My financial situation improved greatly over what it had been. I had a girlfriend, the daughter of a dentist, with whom I spent every spare moment.

A popular girl within the hip social group, she guided me through protocols and behaviors necessary for acceptance. Being her boyfriend brought me many new and exciting experiences unfamiliar to me, including a very exciting session of spin-the-bottle and an enchanting boat ride on the Potomac. Josephine, sophisticated and attractive, knew just how to behave. The group accepted us as a couple, thanks to her patient tutelage and leadership.

We went to several parties, at the last one of which I committed the unforgivable blunder: Another girl asked me if I could walk her home. I took her literally, and walked her the seven or eight blocks to her home and walked immediately back to the party. A very upset Josephine greeted me. In my naivete, I did not understand what she was upset about. The party ending, Josephine coolly informed me that she would walk home with friends. I went home in confusion, not knowing that I had breached some cardinal rule of etiquette. In time, I convinced Josephine that I had not been unfaithful to her.

Life settled down into pleasant rounds of school, work after school and on weekends. Homework, an occasional movie, a trip to the park, with Josephine, or a brief visit at her home, rounded out a very pleasant routine. I still lived in one room with my brother, and we took our meals at the boarding house.

My idyll was interrupted abruptly. I was forced to leave Dunbar towards the beginning of my final semester. Sylvia, four years older than I was, joined us from Tampa, to attend Miner Teachers College. We managed the operation logistically, by moving to a larger room and by providing for privacy by hanging a sheet across the middle of the room at bedtime. My earnings, then about twelve dollars or so per week, made a substantial contribution for food, rent, and the necessities.

Sylvia did not make it for long in the hard cold winter of the North. Tuberculosis seized her, probably contracted by exposure to our father first, and to our brother Raúl only three years previously. She had a full-blown lesion on one of her lungs. She was hospitalized immediately in Gallinger Hospital, which included Washington's sanitarium for patients with tuberculosis.

In connection with Sylvia's hospitalization, I was examined in a public health clinic, a mandatory requirement for anyone shown to be in contact with an active case of tuberculosis. The findings were not conclusive, but the doctors thought they saw a "mottling" on the X-ray of my lung, indicating a possible incipient case of tuberculosis. They ordered me to stop attending Dunbar immediately, and recommended that I seek admittance to the sanitarium also. Shortly thereafter I joined my sister as a patient at Gallinger Hospital. I was to remain under observation for four months.

In June, Miss Brooks, the vice-principal, brought my diploma to the hospital. My happy days at Dunbar had come to an end. Only in the perspective of years have I come to realize what a great loss it was to have missed my high-school graduation. A panoply of rich memories, memories upon which people feed emotionally throughout life, is missing for me. It is as though some vital part of my person has been amputated.

CHAPTER 12

The Thurmans

SHE STOOD IN THE DOORWAY, one of the most beautiful women I had ever met. Richly olive-skinned, small-framed, almost petite, a crown of jet-black hair, an inviting smile, grace and charm itself. Her soft, sweet, full voice enchanted me as she called out, "Do come in. I have been looking forward to meeting you since Henry told me that you would visit."

She has always said that I bowed deeply, and she has attributed that bow to an unusual sense of courtesy on my part. While I had been taught at St. Peter Claver's to bow slightly when speaking to adults, I know now that that bow did not express simple courtesy. Rather, it expressed deference to a unique, powerful presence in a transforming moment that was determining to my life thereafter.

"Helen Wells is going to France for a year of study, and you're going to help me with the jello and the whipped cream for her bon voyage party." Or, "It's Delaney's birthday and I picked up some ginger ale and ice cream to celebrate it. Would you like to help me serve it?" With such simple steps she would turn the slightest opportunity into a celebration and a learning experience.

What Mrs. Sue Thurman did was to give of herself to young people. With little money, she would arrange a party in nothing flat. With three large bottles of ginger ale, a quart of vanilla ice cream, and six students to share in the festivity, she had the makings for a birthday party.

Bon Voyage parties required slightly more preparation: six bottles of ginger ale, three boxes of blue or green jello, a half-pint of cream to whip up waves, toothpicks, and two sheets of white bond paper to make the sails. In short order we would have the table display of boats sailing the ocean. The honorees usually wept at such special treatment!

Mrs. Thurman gave of herself to me by the frequent and special talks we had planning my future. Every talk I had with her lighted pathways to my past and lifted my vision of what my future could be.

I appeared at her door on a hot Saturday in July, about four weeks after I arrived in Washington from Tampa. My brother Henry and I had moved up Georgia Avenue to Gresham Place, near Howard University. Henry had come to know her during the year that he had been a student at Bethune Cookman College, in Daytona Beach, which he had attended by supporting himself by working as a grounds person. Mrs. Thurman visited Bethune Cookman in the course of her annual tour of the black colleges in the southern section of the country, as the National Student Secretary of the YWCA.

She was married to Dr. Howard Thurman, newly appointed Dean of the Chapel at Howard University. She brought Henry into the circle of young people that constantly surrounded the couple. Through Sue, Henry came to know Howard, a towering influence in our lives and in the lives of thousands of students at Howard University and at colleges and universities throughout the country where he lectured.

It was an important moment in my social and psychological development as a black American. I became a part of not merely a black American home, but a black upper-class family, one at the very center of black American intellectual life and very prominent in larger American religious circles. Dr. Thurman's position as dean of the prestigious Rankin Chapel, his fame as a great preacher, and Mrs. Thurman's own stature as a founding member of the National Council of Negro Women all made it that simple.

I did not live with the Thurmans. But I was at their home almost daily, doing some chore that they had cooked up to keep me close to them, or simply interacting with the college students who were always coursing through their home. One summer, Henry and I lived in their home while they were on a trip to India.

Mrs. Thurman led me into the foyer of the home, and then into the living room. It was moment of great wonder for me: wonder at the beauty and elegance of the setting, at the rugs, the highly polished floors, the paintings, the deeply upholstered furnishings. But primarily I wondered at this graceful, warm, woman who had so effortlessly taken me into her life.

She sat down beside me, asked a few gentle questions, and then said, "We're so glad you came to Washington. You'll do well here. We'll keep and eye on you and we'll help in ways that we can. You seem to be a fine young man. Come by whenever you wish."

Located next to Clarke Hall, a large dormitory for men, the Thurman home was a mecca for both students and young visiting faculty members from other historically black colleges, especially religious leaders who came to speak at Andrew Rankin Chapel. Always, the Thurmans had two students living with them. This was a rich environment, indeed, for a boy of fifteen, only weeks away from the barren streets of Tampa.

I had limited opportunity to visit the Thurmans during the summer, for I was busy with my odd jobs, caddying at Chevy Chase Country Club or selling peanuts and sodas at Griffith Stadium. In September, however, I began to pass by their house on the way back home from high school. They sometimes were out doors, perhaps swinging slowly on the glider that sat in the side yard. They would invite me in for a brief chat before I continued on to my way home across Georgia Avenue about five blocks away.

"How's school, Evelio? Dunbar is one of the best high schools in the country, you know. How are you making it? Do you find the work difficult?"

"I believe that I am doing well but I never studied so hard in my life."

"That's fine! You'll be good and ready for college when you finish. I am sure that you will do well."

As fall descended, and it was no longer possible to sit in the open, the Thurmans invited me in to visit with them or simply to sit in the music room and read or talk with one or another of the visiting students. I soon began to do odd jobs for them, polishing the brass, waxing floors, keeping the yards neat, and the like. I now realize that polishing the brass was a never-ending task, just the thing to keep me close, yet out of their hair.

I came to know many of the intellectual leaders of black America in the Thurman home. Ralph Bunche, future Secretary General of the United Nations, shared the duplex in which the Thurmans lived. I had a simple hello and goodbye relationship with him. Dr. Melvin Watson, Professor of Religion at Dillard and Morehouse Universities was part of the family. A protege of Dr. Thurman, he spent blocks of time in the home. We called him "Uncle Monk." Dr. Ernest Everett Just, the world-ranked biologist, I remember most vividly because he would sit at his window waiting for me to come by after school for what became our daily chat.

"How'd it go today, young feller? Too bad your team lost Friday."

"Yeah, I thought we would win that one."

He would be dressed in a T-shirt, as though this was his relaxation hour. I never met him up close, but we really enjoyed our daily chats. One of my other favorites was Rayford Logan, the great historian. He was matter-of-fact and very simple, and he treated me casually. We talked a lot of baseball.

An extraordinary man, Dr. Thurman, like Sue, made me a member of the family. Though busy with his teaching, with the steady stream of students and visitors who made the Thurman home their center, and with preparation for his brilliant sermons, he made time for me whenever I sought him out for a word or two of advice. Much of the time we were engaged in the banter that accompanies simple living together.

In succession, he was Dean of the Andrew Rankin Memorial Chapel at Howard University, founder and pastor of Fellowship Church in San Francisco, and Dean of Marsh Chapel of Boston University. He later founded the Howard Thurman Educational Trust in San Francisco. He authored twenty-three books, which enjoy brisk sales to this day. He was named by *Life* magazine as one of America's twelve greatest preachers.

He spoke with a transfixing eloquence. He had an awe-inspiring command of the English language. He was understood by most people, for his sermons expressed feeling eloquently, were lucid and, above all, were poetic. He managed always to involve his audiences as he wove, with his expressive face, piercing eyes, and gracefully moving arms and body, a passage in a sermon that had vital meaning for him. He would struggle almost painfully as he introduced a theme, insisting that his auditors struggle with him for understanding. Once assured that the congregation was fully with him, he poured forth a waterfall of language, beautiful, ethereal, profoundly moving.

He was a large, very dark man, a powerful, inviting presence. He moved his whole body with a light arresting grace, that complemented fully the beauty of his language and the music of his speech. His deep, melodic voice surrounded and enveloped the congregation, held by the sheer power of his presentation. While he projected himself as the deeply spiritual man that he was, his every sermon was also an exercise in virtuoso theater.

Mine was the privilege of knowing the Thurmans up close, of having them as teachers, of having them care for me as for a son. They were fully conscious of their role, constantly expanding my vision of the possibilities which existed for me.

During one quiet talk, Mrs. Thurman listened to me think out loud about career choices. I had begun to visualize myself in different capacities and on this occasion I spoke about becoming a lawyer. Mrs. Thurman did not hesitate one second. "You have a fine mind. You are doing very well in school. Your use of English is excellent. You speak Spanish fluently. Why not consider the opportunities you may have as a diplomat?"

I felt a surge of excitement, although I had no idea as to how one prepared one self to become a diplomat. I had never even thought of myself as being part of the world of diplomacy. I walked away from the Thurman home that evening with a completely new concept of myself and of what was possible with an education. The limits were suddenly pushed out a little farther for me.

At the beginning of my senior year in high school I talked to Dr. Thurman about college, asking what I needed to do to get into Howard University. He was almost impatient with me.

"You are not going to Howard," he said sharply and emphatically. "It's too cold up here and you are too poor. Housing will cost you more, and you'll need warmer, more expensive clothing. You are going to Xavier University, in New Orleans. I believe that they will want you there, and that they will find ways to help you finance your schooling."

I had never heard of Xavier, a Catholic college for blacks in New Orleans. Never mind, the issue was settled then and there. "Doctor T," as we called him, had spoken, and for those of us whom he made his children, that settled the matter. I made application, and arranged for the transcript of my record at Dunbar to be sent to Xavier. But no answer came from the college.

About three weeks before the beginning of the semester, I began to worry and I brought my worries to Dr. T. He thought a moment, and then, wondering out loud, asked, "Have you met any Xavier graduates?"

It happened that I had sought out and had been talking to Archie Lecesne and Vincent Malveaux, Xavier graduates, who were attending the Howard University School of Law. "Go talk with them. Ask their advice." he suggested.

I did so that very morning. Lecesne and Malveaux lived on Georgia Avenue, just three blocks away. I went to the rooming house where they lived and found them at home, studying. They welcomed me warmly and helped me enormously.

"Sister Madeleine Sophie [the Dean] happens to be in Washington at this time," Lescesne informed me.

"Why don't you try to reach her?" Malveaux added.

I hurried back to Dr. T with the news. He asked me immediately, "Did you get her phone number?" I had not, of course. "You run back there and get it," he commanded, urgently.

I ran to and from Archie and Vincent's place. I gave him the number. He called it immediately. Reaching Sister Madeleine Sophie, he spoke to her in his deep, rich, sonorous voice. "I am very happy to speak with you, Sister. This is Howard Thurman, Dean of the Chapel of Howard University. I have a young man here with me who is going to Xavier University." He said it with a finality that made it clear that the only matters left to discuss were the arrangements that would make it possible for a penniless young man to matriculate at Xavier.

Sister Madeleine Sophie was apparently touched, for, after he told her a few things about me, the rest of the phone discussion was given to a friendly chat between them about education, and about the importance of providing opportunities for youth seeking to enter college. During the discussion he managed to make an appointment for me to see Sister at the convent at three o'clock that very afternoon.

The rest is denouement. I appeared at the convent at three o'clock promptly. Sister Madeleine Sophie, a large, impressive woman who behaved as though comfortable with power, ushered me into a parlor where about fifteen young people were gathered, all a little older than I. They were Xavier alumni, come to visit with the Dean during her brief stay in Washington. I sat and listened to the discussion as the alumni brought Sister up to date. They told her about their work, their graduate studies, their organizational activities, their marriages, and their children.

At a certain point, Sister arose and said, "Well, young people, it is time for my prayers, so I must send you on your way." All arose and formed a line to take leave from Sister one by one.

I was puzzled, but I assumed that what Sister had to say to me she would say during the leave taking, so I assumed the last place in the line. As I approached Sister, she extended her hand as though she were saying goodbye to me also. Now panicked, I said nervously, "Sister, I am Evelio Grillo, the young man whom Dr. Thurman discussed with you this morning."

A light went on in Sister's mind. Then she puzzled for a bit. Then she said to me, almost as an afterthought, "You get yourself down to Xavier, and when you get there ask to see Mother Pierre. We'll see each other in about a week when I return from my trip." She shook my hand warmly, smiled broadly, and ushered me out the door. It was clear that her primary concern was to be on time for prayers.

It was that simple. I had no idea at the time, but Sister Madeleine Sophie had just awarded me a four-year scholarship, covering tuition and all fees, and had given me a job to cover the costs of room and board.

CHAPTER 13

Xavier University

EVEN IN A CITY WHERE impressive structures abound, the Washington Union Railway Station distinguished itself. Huge, imposing, it sat, a brooding sentinel, guarding the entrance to the capital of a nation perhaps the most powerful on earth. It beckoned all to consider the grandeur of the city they were entering or leaving.

This hub of travel occupies a prominent place in the scheme of the city. Its enormous portals pour into a marbled-floored chamber, which to me seemed as long and as wide as a football field. Green columns, again of marble, swept upward to meet a great expanse of iron-webbed glass, a skylight that seemed six stories away at least.

It covered the dome, almost, and shot shafts of light through the chamber, the shafts catching reflected gleams, as they bathed the myriad of particles of dust that floated in the station's atmosphere.

Rushes of activity went on at any hour of the day. They became somewhat less frenetic after only midnight. All throughout the floor of the building, streams of people moved to and from the trains, taxis, autos, and buses. The people resembled trails of ants, foraging for food and storing provisions.

On a cold morning in January 1937, I became one of the ants. Heading out with high hopes for New Orleans and Xavier, I walked rapidly across the acres of floor, out the portal leading to the trains, and past the white conductor, who, studiously and contemptuously avoiding my gaze, directed me into the "Jim Crow" car.

Our nation's capital was one of the transfer points where black passengers were forced to change from non-segregated to segregated trains. Blacks underwent this ceremony of denigration every time we traveled by railway going from north to south and crossed the Mason-Dixon line.

Father. Antonio Grillo, in a photograph taken during the early 1920s.

Family. The Grillos circa 1920. From left: Sylvia, Raúl, Evelio (in mother's lap), Amparo Grillo, Henry, and Anival.

Mother. Amparo Grillo in the early 1930s.

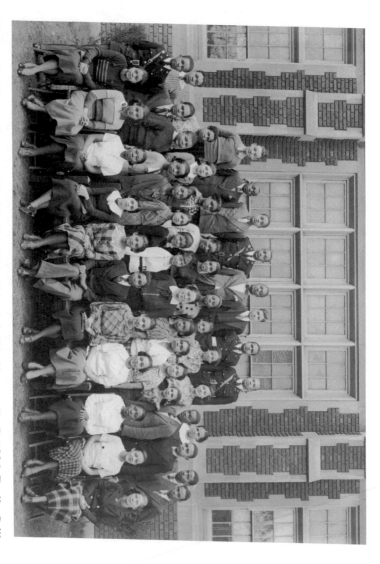

Up North. The student council of Dunbar High School, in Washington, D. C, 1936. Evelio Grillo, president, sits at the center of the front row.

School. The college student,
memorizing lines for a student play.
Xavier University, New Orleans,
circa 1938.

At War. In his U. S. Army uniform, 1942. The photograph is signed, *"A Berta y Anival con todo el cariño de Evelio."*

Back in the States. The Grillo clan (except for sister Sylvia, in Florida) in Washington, D.C., in 1947. Back row, from left: Evelio, brothers Henry and Anival. Front row, with children: Catherine (wife of Evelio); Altagracia (wife of Henry); Amparo Grillo; and Berta (wife of Anival).

Service. Evelio Grillo, Executive Assistant for Policy Development at the U.S. Department of Health, Education, and Welfare, meets President Jimmy Carter in 1978. *(Official White House photograph)*

The car "for colored" was placed near the front of the train, behind the baggage car, and the railway mail cars. We thought it was the oldest and the least comfortable the railway company could muster. It smelled and had a shabby appearance.

On one of my trips to New Orleans, the "colored" car had no air-conditioning. The windows had small mesh screens through which the humidity flowed into the car, mixed with the soot that belched from the engine. The mixture soiled our clothes, and made messes of our hands, arms, necks, and faces. We made frequent trips to the bathroom to wash the filth away.

The kitchen car and the dining car, where the waiters served elegant meals, sat behind the "colored" car, forming a separation between "colored" and white passengers. As I recall it, black passengers could eat in the dining car after all white passengers had been served.

We struggled with our carry-on luggage. Many black travelers carried the ubiquitous shoeboxes filled with crispy fried chicken, a tradition for blacks coming from or going to the Deep South. Celery sticks, raw carrots, fresh-baked rolls, pound cake, and cookies would supplement the chicken in some boxes. A "traveler's shoebox" came as a welcome gift from friends and relatives.

Finally, all passengers settled, we began to notice one another. The train moved more rapidly over the rails now, picking up the speed to carry it to Atlanta, the transfer point between Washington and New Orleans. I met older men who conversed with me, usually encouraging me to stick with college. I had no idea that I would draw this much attention just on the basis of how I acted. Not many students were traveling, this being the height of the Depression, with trips home an unaffordable luxury.

Some passengers made modest overtures to demonstrate their appreciation and support of students attending college. One elderly lady surprised me with a large piece of chicken, a roll, a cookie, and an apple, all tendered with kindness and a smile: "Here, young man, this will hold you for a while. I hope you enjoy it." I thanked her gratefully. We sat together for a while and exchanged pleasant conversation. My first railway trip had developed into a very enjoyable social experience.

As darkness descended, we began to make preparations for the long night's ride into Atlanta. Some passengers left the train at Atlanta. Some others joined us. A scramble went on for the available seats. But soon all was in order and we assumed the most comfortable positions we could manage. Eventually, the lights lowered, passengers began to catch a little sleep.

Merciful dawn eventually crept through the windows. The car became alive with activity. We lined up to use the restrooms to wash our hands and faces, and to straighten out our clothes. When the time came, a few went into the dining car for breakfast.

We got our luggage in order. Our railway adventure nearly over, we took our leave of one another, promising to phone, to write, or to drop by if ever we visited the particular person's vicinity. Half-hearted gestures all, for we busied ourselves recovering our baggage excitedly and planning our transportation to our respective destinations.

Hurrying to get to the Xavier campus, I asked around for directions. One gentleman directed me to the trolley car that took me to Xavier with just one transfer. After my two and one-half years of greater racial freedom in Washington, sadly, I had to return to the indignity of sitting in the rear section of the car behind a FOR COLORED ONLY sign.

(Among my first lessons in defiance as a neophyte Xavierite, the upper classmen admonished me that it was my duty to steal one of these demeaning signs and to nail it to the wall over my bed. This was easy to do. One balmy night, when the windows of the trolley were open, I sat quietly behind a sign and, as the vehicle approached Xavier, I slipped the sign off the seat and threw it out of the window. After I got off the trolley, I walked back to pick up the sign and walked triumphantly to The Big House, our dormitory, where I received a noisy welcome from my athlete friends.)

I reached the corner of Washington and Palmetto streets, made famous by Xavier. I walked over the bridge that crossed the wide concrete-lined flood canal that ran the full length of Washington Street, the very front of the university. Two suitcases in hand, in a black formal overcoat, a thin dark blue summer suit, and a new dark blue cap, I must have been a curious sight. I had no awareness of looking odd, but I later discovered that the students mistook me for a seminarian who had either been bounced from the seminary or quit voluntarily.

Entering the campus, I gazed in awe at this stately large building. Standing alone, without even a single tree to keep it company, a crucifix mounted at its pinnacle, it stood majestically. Made of expensive granite, with many gothic features, it clearly stood as a landmark of a religious institution.

I climbed the massive stairs at the front center of the structure, only to find that the heavy, highly polished doors were locked. Turning back, I followed the sidewalk to the right and walked around the corner, where I met a couple of friendly faces. They kept their distance, possibly out of respect for someone who, they assumed, had just left the seminary. They didn't ask me a single question, and I, intimidated by their silence, said nothing also. A much smaller door led into the building.

Soon I reached the Registrar's Office, where confusion attended my arrival. The registrar, a kind, sweet lady named Mrs. Gabriel, had no knowledge of my coming.

I said to her, "Sister Madeleine Sophie told me to look up Mother Pierre as soon as I got here."

"She did?" replied Mrs. Gabriel, relieved to have some clue about the mystery of my arriving so undocumented.

"Let's call the cafeteria, they may know something down there," she said. A call to Mother Pierre, who ran the cafeteria with an iron hand, was all that it took.

"Someone's coming to get you," said Mrs. Gabriel, "and then we'll find out everything. Meanwhile I wish you a happy and successful stay at Xavier, Mr. Grillo. I'm sure I'll be seeing you soon," she said, kindly.

A pleasant young man soon came by to pick me up. It turned out to be a prophetic encounter. Lawrence "Mike" Thomas, as it developed, became my bunkmate in the room that the five of us who worked in the kitchen shared in "The Big House." A huge, old converted Victorian, "The Big House" served as lodging for athletes, the vast majority of whom were football players.

Mike also became my best friend. Older than I, he was quiet and sensitive. Nothing would interfere with the bond we forged. We became as loving brothers. We remained roommates throughout our entire stay at Xavier.

Dropping off my suitcases, we rushed over to the cafeteria to meet Sister Ancilla, Mother Pierre's able assistant. She greeted me warmly. "We knew you were coming, but we didn't know when. Are you hungry? Mother Pierre said you were to take it easy this afternoon getting your things unpacked and settling in your room. Then come over with the boys for dinner. You don't have to work tonight. Come in tomorrow morning at five o'clock, ready to help prepare and to serve breakfast. Come in at four o'clock in the afternoon to help prepare and to serve supper."

"I'll be here, Sister Ancilla. Please thank Mother Pierre for me, and please say to her that I am looking forward very much to working in the cafeteria," I responded. We parted with a firm handshake. Quickly, I gathered the impression that everyone shook with fear when Mother Pierre spoke.

In awe, I experienced this all as unbelievable. So! That's how I was going to pay for my room and board! I could not have been happier; lodging and board would be provided in exchange for my work in the kitchen and dining room. The luckiest man on earth, that's the way I figured it.

There was more to come! To pay for my lunch, on school days, I came in at noon and served the professors: sandwiches, soup, desserts, milk, chocolate, coffee, and soft drinks of all kinds. The professors taken care of, I had about twenty minutes to get my own lunch.

At one o'clock it was back to classes, and at three o'clock it was practice for whatever play, oratorical contest, or opera was coming up next. During that semester, I won the oratorical contest and played the title role in the morality play *Everyman.* I was enjoying myself tremendously.

Highly motivated to study, I put in at least four hours a day, mostly from seven to eleven at night, and during weekends. We had to work only the breakfast and lunch meals on Sundays. We were then given a bag lunch, consisting of a roast beef sandwich, a piece of fruit, and a pint carton of milk.

Breakfast was hilarious. Only a genius of the kitchen could have done it. Mother Pierre purchased at least fourteen rolled round roasts for those roast beef sandwiches we ate on Sundays. The beef was boiled in two fifteen-gallon pots. After letting them cool, James, the leader of our kitchen crew, would take the roasts out of the pots and set the oozing masses on grates to drain. The rich, heavy, liquid would be combined into one pot and placed in the large refrigerator, where it would be safe from spoiling.

James' first chore upon arriving in the mornings would be to brown flour by literally burning it in an immense iron skillet. He then heated some of the rendered beef stock saved from the boiling of the round roasts. He stirred the flour constantly until it assumed a uniform, deep, golden brown color. To this mass of flour, he slowly added the hot beef stock until a tasty gravy was formed. Poured over big plates of hot grits, and served with hot whole-wheat toast and a piece of fruit, the "miracle" provided a filling, nutritious starter for the day.

The meal did become monotonous, but from my point of view, at least, the regularity and the fact that the meals cost me nothing out of pockets that were empty, gave me a sense of appreciation for those oft-maligned grits and gravy.

The entire semester passed for me rapidly. Fully engaged, I enjoyed the time of my life, what with the opera chorus, the concert choir, the oratorical competition, and the play.

Moreover, I was making a host of new friends. Skeegee, the most interesting of the lot, had transferred in from Tuskeegee University in Alabama, hence his nickname. He came from Geechees, a subset of blacks who were some how related to the French, I believe. They had a distinctive accent.

Short and nondescript, Skeegee had a great sense of humor and became a very popular student. Most importantly, he was a serious scholar of French and he became fluent in the language. He played the leading role in Moliere's *Le Bourgeois Gentilhomme*. Frankly envious of him, I admired the way Skeegee played the role and I knew that I would not have done half as well in it. As one of life's rewards, I found a good friend in Skeegee. He joined Mike, Terry, Howard and me as roommates.

Terry Francois, at nineteen the youngest of our class, did not compete for honors, but his classmates respected him as the most brilliant one among us. He went on to earn a master's degree in political science from Atlanta University, and, ultimately, a law degree from Hastings College of the Law. He became the first black member of the San Francisco Board of Supervisors, where he had an illustrious career.

Time had once again played its trick on us, and we were saying good-bye to the graduates and "see you later" to those returning in the fall. We would miss them more than we realized.

I rushed back to Washington—to work profitably, I thought. Dr. Bernard King, a dentist who was the father of Josephine, my steady girlfriend in high school, found me a job as a busboy in Saratoga Springs, New York, during the thirty-day racing season. Everybody expected to make a killing. We were mightily disappointed, for only a few racing fans showed up, and very little money flowed.

The fiasco must have disoriented me, for nothing but catastrophes visited me the rest of the summer. On one errand, I lost the vest to my headwaiter's tuxedo while on the way to the cleaners. I can still remember his dismayed look when he said to me, "How does one manage to lose a vest?" I left Dr. Thurman's doctoral gown on the trolley on the way back from the cleaners. Dr. Thurman could only shake his head and breathe a deep sigh of quiet desperation. I set fire to my brother's house while attempting to fumigate a steamer trunk I had purchased for five dollars at the local Salvation Army store.

Having survived all these tragedies, my self-esteem sorely diminished, I wanted very much to return to the routine and security of Xavier.

My hopes of saving a bundle by working during the summer had been dashed. First, the Saratoga job yielded only twenty-five dollars, and much of what I earned in Washington—fifty dollars or so—I gave to Dr. Thurman to compensate for what must have been a major loss for him.

I arrived at Xavier that September, weary, disappointed, disheveled, and fearful that if I initiated anything, it surely would come to a disastrous end. But I soon discovered, to my surprise, that I would no longer be working in the cafeteria. A spot had been found for me in the NYA program. President Roosevelt had established the National Youth Administration, in part, to finance part-time jobs for college students. I was to earn fifteen dollars monthly, which was enough to pay for my room and board (twelve dollars) and leave me three dollars for incidentals.

Then, on the way back from lunch, I ran into Sister Elise, the head of the music department. Her face, always pleasant and peaceful, shone with a radiance that encouraged others to soften the tone of their speech, so as to be more in tune with her. Her eyes glowed with affection for each of her students. Fortune placed me in the path of their gaze at that moment.

She was a remarkably skilled musician. She had the voice of a Metropolitan Opera mezzo soprano, rich, deep. It was whispered that she, a highly trained and educated professional opera singer, gave up a successful career to enter the Sisters of the Blessed Sacrament. Its wealthy founder, Blessed (Mother) Katherine Drexel, had organized the order specifically for the education of "Indians and Colored People"; she was ultimately scheduled by Pope John Paul II to be canonized as a saint of the Catholic Church in the year 2000.

Sister Elise was superbly versed in music. She made opera a vital element in the Xavier community, and extended its reach deep into the New Orleans community. Besides her trained dramatic talent, she manifested passion, passion that uplifted her students and that helped us to do our best at all times. Sister Elise made my college experience joyous and my attitudes towards my studies and work positive and optimistic. Her soft smile, manner of speech, and always encouraging words built my confidence. She worked very hard to bring out the best in each of us. As though it were yesterday, I can see her face aglow, her arms moving gracefully, yet vigorously, as she directed the great choruses that she developed.

The great spiritual "Listen To The Lambs" always comes to mind whenever I reminisce over the happy experiences singing in the choir. Sister Elise led us to feel the pain and the sadness that the song elicited.

Well known in the African American Opera community, she played the leading role in organizing the National Ebony Opera. Within its context many nationally celebrated African Americans performed their art. While at Xavier she produced a major opera each year. Mine was the privilege of singing in the opera chorus. *Tales of Hoffman* and *Carmen* were my favorites.

A brief encounter in the hallway became of great significance in my development. I can remember every aspect of it clearly. Sister Elise spoke to me earnestly, but, as always, with the slightest smile on her face and a twinkle in her eye. "Young man, I have a matter of some importance to discuss with you. I would like to have you work with me. Would you like to work for me? I would like that very much."

Dumbfounded by Sister Elise's words, I hardly knew what to say. Merely a member of the chorus, not a music major, Sister Elise's offer surprised and delighted me. I thought she was the most outstanding member of the faculty.

I responded, "I feel honored to be asked to work for you. All I need to know is what my job will be and when I am to start."

"For the present, let's say your job is to get situated. Find a place to stay. Sign up for your classes and make the adjustments that always are necessary. Arrange for your meals. Above all, spend some time with the friends you have made and the new ones you will meet; that's very important. Then, in about two weeks, when you are settled, come to the music department and we will discuss your job," she closed, with the greatest aplomb imaginable, as though she were discussing a routine assignment.

I took my astonished leave of Sister Elise with a handshake. She had imbedded herself into my spirit.

She intervened in my life at a crucial time, as I entered my young adult years full of spirit, ideas, plans, ambitions. Without ever mentioning the word, she led me to realize more fully that love is the key factor in life.

I visited Sister Elise infrequently after I left Xavier, wherever she was stationed, and I wrote to her much less often than I should have. But she and I know the fullness of my love for her, and of my gratitude for her gift of love to me.

I went looking for Mike immediately to tell him the good news. He, too, was bubbly. "Dr. Paytash gave me job in the chemistry lab," he gushed, with more animation than he usually displayed. "Man! I'll have time to really study now!" Mike firmly intended to become a dentist. His determination inspired us all.

We went looking for Terry Francois, Howard, and Skeegee, with whom we had had discussions about rooming together. I already had spotted a house large enough for us all. The landlady was apparently pleasant, and so we very quickly made arrangements to move in at four dollars each per month.

For meals we decided to try "Mom's" Capillon. Mom's provided a large plate of rice and beans and an occasional piece of chicken or pork chops, all for eight dollars a month. So we signed up. Thus launched, we turned to the business of buying books and supplies.

Promptly at four o'clock, as we had arranged it two weeks previously, I arrived at the music department for my appointment with Sister Elise. Silhouetted in black, she floated down the hall towards me.

I had my private name for the sisters who walked the halls during the day. Some I called dashers, because they were the smaller ones with short legs, who had to dash to cover the distances they had to walk. Others I termed gallopers. Every part of their bodies was involved when they walked, their arms, their lower limbs, their heads. Sister Elise was a floater. She moved effortlessly and at the most moderate pace through the halls. We walked arm in arm into the music rooms, and we went into the center rear room, where Sister Elise took her place on the piano bench and I sat on a folding chair opposite her.

"So you want to know what your job will be," Sister opened, with that same quiet smile, as always, in place. "I will tell you now." Then she said, with firmness, "Your job is to educate yourself! Take advantage of every thing the university offers. Take part in everything your schedule allows. If you are in the midst of rehearsal for a play or an opera or in choir practice don't interrupt what you are doing to come and clean the music rooms. What you do makes a substantial contribution to the university. It should be recognized as a contribution, even as football, basketball, tennis and track are recognized. Now, that settled, we can talk about your duties in the music department."

"I would like that," I said, pleased to get a word in, for Sister Elise had rendered me speechless.

"Well, I would sweep and dust these three music rooms. The furniture should be put back in order each day. The plants should be kept moist also, so perhaps you should check them to see if they need water."

"Is that all?" The tasks as outlined did not seem to require more than an hour and a half of work.

"That will be more than enough for a busy student like you; but there's one more item that we can take care of when we can. Once a month you and I should put on some working rags on a Saturday morning and give the place a good waxing. I think that will be enough don't you? Then there'll be little unexpected things we can't foresee, errands and the like. What do you say we call this an agreement?"

More than pleased, I let her know so. Sister then terminated the session with the usual, "It's time for my prayers."

The conversation effectively closed, we walked side by side through those beautiful halls until we were near the passageway that led to the convent. A handshake and loving words ended the encounter.

Now completely settled, I turned my attention to serious study, under the guidance of great dedicated teachers. Dr. Bouise, my English professor, would accept nothing but my best work. One time I brought my work to him only to hear him say, "I believe that I would be unfair if I did not assign an A to this composition. The only question remaining is whether you will accept an A for what obviously is not your best work."

Frustrated and disappointed, I took the composition back, reworked it carefully, and returned it to hear him say, "Now *that's* an A paper!"

Miss Charlotte Merot, another brilliant professor, taught me French. To write *taught* is to do dishonor to what she did. She immersed me in French. Her vehicle was the annual French play, through which she had all of us striving to pronounce the language correctly. Tall, lithe, with a mop of light brown hair, she presided over her French Empire with a contagious smile and sweet manner. She achieved her goals. She gave others and me hours of individual tutoring.

Notwithstanding its rich offerings in music and drama, Xavier was most widely known for its athletics. It had powerful football teams, championship basketball teams, and nationally ranked tennis and track stars. These teams and players were widely known and respected in black college circles.

Thus it went for me during the four years I spent at Xavier, except for the antipathy I aroused in some faculty members because I was self-centered and insufferably cocksure.

In the early days, Mother Pierre, who was well practiced in dealing with prima donnas, brought this dramatically to my attention. I had received an encouraging letter from the philosopher Alain Locke, for whom I had worked in Washington, receiving orders and mailing his books. The letter made me very happy, and, in my enthusiasm, I showed it to Mother Pierre. During my next pass by the table where she sat supervising the cafeteria, she handed me back the letter and said, "I think you may be the most self-centered person I have known."

That took the wind out of my sails. At first I was angry and thought that Mother Pierre had no appreciation of Alain Locke. But as the days passed, I recognized the conceit in my attitude. Humility did not distinguish my demeanor, which, in the perspective of the years, makes sense, since I must have been one of the most insecure students on the campus. I believe Mother

Pierre became fonder of me as the years passed, but not fond enough to forget the letter and what it said about me.

Four years passed rapidly in a whirlwind of studies, classes, work, operas, concerts, plays, football games, basketball games, track meets, tennis championship matches, elaborate sacred ceremonies, and the one dance a year I could afford. All in all, I enjoyed an arduous but pleasant time. But the storm clouds were gathering, nonetheless. In the last semester of my senior year they struck with a vengeance.

I had developed a reputation as social activist of sorts. For example, I led the fund drive for the victims of a large fire that had destroyed a large ballroom in Natchez, Mississippi, with a large loss of lives. I was criticized by Sister Madeline, a very powerful nun, for making my appeal too blatant with respect to racial pride.

"Race had nothing to do with it," she held. "The issue is only confused with the banners appealing to racial pride."

I have thought of this incident often, since it seemed to loom large in my college career. My position was that the ballroom was a deathtrap, and that the great loss of life could have been averted by proper zoning laws, which were, apparently, notoriously insufficient in black neighborhoods. As I have grown in understanding and knowledge of love, however, I have come to realize that Sister Madeline, for all her seeming rigidities, had a point. There may have been something to be desired in the way she dealt with me, but in the perspective of years, that does not seem as important either.

Nonetheless, we chose up sides on controversial issues. I had made it clear that I was not subject to "de-Negrofication," a term that many will understand who have served on the margins of powerful white institutions. I reserved the right to "think black," and to "feel black," on social issues, whatever the circumstances.

In the last part of my senior year, I became seriously involved in an activity that gave the administration substantial concern, and which brought me to the attention of a largely disapproving college community. The Southern Negro Youth Congress, which many believed was a Communist-front organization, held its convention in New Orleans. I had not been active in community organizations while in college. So I answered the call for volunteers to work as assistants during the convention. Our responsibilities were to register delegates, to prepare the rooms for discussion groups, and to prepare handouts and other materials. There were white students from surrounding colleges, as well as white adults helping to prepare for the convention.

This completely new experience made me apprehensive, for I knew instinctively that there was something amiss about a situation in which white and blacks were working together closely and cooperatively, not too mention that they were socializing, yet! The matter became clear for me in the bull sessions held after work was done at night. That's when the Guru—one of the Congress's leaders—would hold court.

Suddenly, the news broke that the Soviets had entered the war against Germany. Immediately the Seamen's International Union declared a "no-strike" pledge. Many blacks opposed the no-strike pledge. The United States had not entered the war. We saw no benefit to be derived from giving up our main point of leverage in the struggle for justice and equal treatment, not only on ships, but also in the industries which relied on shipping. Yet here sat this black man defending the no-strike pledge. I developed a strong dislike for the Guru and for the Southern Negro Youth Congress, which, on the basis of what I had heard and seen, I, too, now firmly believed to be a Communist front.

It felt strange, being suspected of Communist leanings on the Xavier campus, and at the same time being held in some contempt at the convention because I was not one of the enthusiastic supporters of the no-strike pledge. But I had strong feelings about both matters, and I held my ground whatever the price. I finished helping with the convention, but with much-diminished enthusiasm and interest. Sorely disappointed, I no longer believed I was working for the black cause.

On the last Sunday evening, after the close of the convention, the Guru and his disciples gathered around me and congratulated me for "having seen the light."

"What light?" I said. "I've seen nothing but darkness around here." With that, I left the group, and made my lonely, weary, and confused way back to the campus. On my return to the campus, I received no smiles or greetings, except from two disaffected students.

The last month of my senior year, I felt angry, not so much for being considered a renegade, but more because I was not trusted in asserting my individuality outside the campus on my own. I received no honors but a *cum laude*. Graduation seemed like a bad dream, with my classmates inquiring, "What happened?" Visibly embarrassed and upset, I had not yet learned to be cool under fire.

In the perspective of the years, however, it is not appropriate or necessary to focus on the negative aspects of my largely pleasant years at Xavier. Xavier took me in, one of many penniless if deserving young people of college age. It provided me with a superb education, which I have used advantageously for my own growth in life, for my family's benefit and, I hope, for the benefit of the many communities that I have served.

Xavier's nuns were legitimately disappointed in me from their perspective. They had invested everything they could in me, and they may have hoped that I would perform more to their expectations. Instead, I was seen by highly placed nuns and by some members of the lay faculty as a rebel. They had a legitimate right to be disappointed—I gave every evidence of no longer practicing the Catholic faith. To the nuns, this was akin to the loss of a son. I remind myself frequently that my college education came about because Mr. Martin and a multitude of others cared enough about what "a southern colored boy can do." But they were complemented at the other end of the line by a college that knew how to love young men and women.

PART THREE

At War

CHAPTER 14

Shoving Off

AFTER FOURTEEN HOURS OF WAITING in line along a wall of the wharf, we saw our ship, the U.S.S. *Santa Paula*. We had no idea where we were going. In keeping with protocols of army secrecy, we had not been told.

Aboard the *Santa Paula* we were to spend fifty-eight dreary days as it carried us to India. While on it, we were to fight the opening battle in the primary war for black U.S. troops in World War II: the war against segregation within the United States Army!

When it was our turn to board the gray, ghostly behemoth, we moved in single file along the gangplank, onto the vessel, and into the hold, the very bottom of the ship. Narrow little sleeping pads awaited us, arranged in stacks of three against both bulkheads.

In the center, rows of triple bunks were arranged to account for every inch of space, while providing narrow aisles for maneuvering between the rows of bunks. The noncommissioned officers, twenty-four in number, had slightly more comfortable arrangements, for we bunked near the equipment that we supervised.

There wasn't a single opening to daylight. We slept below the water line. We could hear the ocean slap constantly against the side of the ship. No forced air ventilation could match the stench cooked up by the sweat, the farts, and the vomit of two hundred men. This was only one of the many indignities inflicted upon us by the complement of white officers who commanded us.

White troops had fresh water for showering. Black troops had to shower with sea water. White troops had the ample stern of the ship to lounge during the day. Black troops were consigned to the narrow bow, so loaded with gear that it was difficult to find comfortable resting places. The sea sloshed over the bow furiously in foul weather, so even that area was unavailable to us when the sea thrashed. At such times we roamed the decks open to black troops until it was our turn to go into the dining halls—for segregated meals.

The vast majority of the men were confined to the foul-smelling hold. Some of us were lucky; we had jobs that carried us topside. We craved the fresh air of the open sea, available only when the bow was not awash with water.

The very best among the officers who commanded us were two older ones. They both hailed from the midwest. They may have been mildly racist, but they were not barbarians, as were the majority. Captain Jarrett, the company commander, spoke slowly, with a midwestern twang. He was clearly overweight and walked slowly. He was bored with it all, and he carried out his duties with no passion.

For Captain Trainor, we felt compassion. He seemed afraid of everything, and approached every project as though his life depended on it. He relied upon his men (an extraordinary group of college graduates, as well as less educated but very bright men), who constituted the engineering brains of the unit, for advice and guidance. He visibly trembled in the presence of our colonel. Lieutenant Colonel Jason D. Leland, the commanding officer of the battalion, a virulent bigot, set the tone for the adversarial relationship between the officers and the men.

Notwithstanding their weaknesses, Captain Jarrett and Captain Trainor treated us with respect and consideration. We had warm feelings about them. All the rest were either raw, young, recent graduates of the "ninety-day-wonder" schools for officers or more seasoned veterans of the regular army, who had a thinly veiled contempt for black troops. They had no points of familiarity with blacks. And, for our part, we assumed that they had been selected to command us because they were deemed to "know how to handle niggers."

We felt the ship pull out of harbor in the middle of the night. Then we were calmed by the smooth, quiet movement of the ship as she got fully under way. At dawn, we rushed to the bow to get our first glimpse of the sea. An astonishing sight it was! Ships were arrayed in the distance as far as the eye could see in every direction. And beyond that, we saw the smoke rising from ships sailing below the horizon. It was an overpowering view. We were part of an immense convoy, including a number of warships assigned for protective escort to the convoy.

Over the next few days, as we familiarized ourselves with the ship, we realized that the arrangements made for us were grossly discriminatory. We were infuriated and depressed, and we felt impotent. Driven by disgust, a few of us noncommissioned officers discussed the injustices and the denigration. We began to discuss ways of protesting the situation. Shorty Roberts, Shep McCants, George Mason, and I formed this tight little group.

"We've got to do something," Shep began.

"Before we go any further," I interrupted, "we'll have to find a safe place to talk." We agreed upon the bow. No one else would be out on such a stormy night.

Soaked by the heavy spray and buffeted by fierce winds, we had trouble even maintaining our balance as the ship pitched and rolled. We barely could see each other in the pitch darkness of the moonless night. Our faces were awash with the stinging spray, leaving the strong taste of salt in our mouths.

Shep was a magnificent man in many ways: tall, lanky, with rich black skin. Intelligent and not much of a conformist, he was nonetheless a respected five-striped leader of construction crews. He was not a profound man, but he was great fun, good-humored, and jolly. He played every card game. One could always find in him an available partner for hearts, gin, or pinochle. The monthly scenario always repeated itself. Within five days after payday, the professional gamblers would sweep every available penny out of the pockets of those willing to risk. The rest of the month, those who had lost everything had the choice between watching the good gamblers play high-stakes games and playing the "fun games," with no money at risk. There were always numbers of willing players. Shep could always be counted to join the group playing for fun about five days into the cycle.

That night, Shep led with, "This is some very heavy shit these motha fuckas are laying on us. I could kill one of the bastards."

Shorty Roberts then contributed his opinion. "If we take this shit without doing something, we have no balls. Whatcha want us to do, Grillo?" He was certain that I could come up with a practical plan.

Shorty, a six-striper, the sergeant major of the battalion, and the ranking noncommissioned officer, was tough, but not overbearing. I believe he was easily the most intelligent man in our unit. His work was above reproach. He did not have an education beyond high school and had not been trained in management techniques, but he ran the headquarters ably and with a firm hand. About six years older than the average of the headquarters staff, he had maturity to show for his years. Shorty had a sense of humor that kept us all in good spirits. A meticulously clean person, he always smelled and looked like he had just taken a shower and had a shave. I was glad to count him among my friends, for with his extensive knowledge of politics and current events, he was an interesting person with whom to converse. He was the closest thing to a buddy that I had. I was second in command to him in the office. We were in constant contact and gave each other solid support.

As the personnel sergeant, I had direct contact with every man in the battalion, maintaining personnel records, making out allotments of pay to their families, and helping with applications for Government Service Life Insurance. Thus I grew to know the men well and vice versa. Deep bonds of camaraderie and respect developed among many of us.

I didn't know the full implications of our meeting like this; I knew only that we were in dangerous waters. Merely gathering to talk bordered on insubordination. Should discussion escalate into overt action, it could be considered mutinous. That was not my intent, and it wasn't the intent of those involved. We simply wanted to protest legitimate grievances in a proper forum, but we could not anticipate the interpretation our officers might place on the facts. Fear seized me. It accompanied me all the while I was involved in this episode.

Shorty persisted, impatiently, "Whatcha thinkin', Grillo? You're smart. If you help us plan, we'll be all right, no matter what happens! What shall we do?"

Now fully aware that they were looking to me, I said firmly, "We're not going to do anything that we don't plan carefully, and we're not going to begin planning anything definite until we seek the support of the rest of the guys."

"Oh, we'll have that," Shep spoke confidently.

"Don't take it for granted!" I countered.

Shorty spoke impatiently again, "Whatcha thinking, Grillo? Whatcha want us to do?" While he insisted that I lead, I was scared to death. "They are not going to give me the shit they give niggers in the south. I'm ready to show 'em here and now," he continued. "Whatcha think we should do, Grillo?" He thereby placed the reins of leadership in my hands.

"We'll divide the list of noncommissioned officers among us equally. We'll ask them individually if they are willing to join a protest of the way we were being treated." I continued, "We'll warn them of the risks, possible demotion, and possible court-martial. If they want to know more, we'll tell them we don't have a plan yet. We are waiting for their approval before proceeding. We want to know how they feel."

George Mason, the company's orderly and mail clerk, silent until then, spoke. George, a corporal, and younger than all of us, may have felt a little over his head. He had listened very intently to this point, but had said nothing. Yet, he was the most enthusiastic about our meeting.

George was very fair of skin, trim, very neat, and well organized. As orderly, he had daily contact with the men. He was the center of communication, and he carried out his duties with pride, great dignity, and with utter trustworthiness. For example, he knew everyone's secrets, joys, and sorrows. He knew when a man received a "Dear John" letter from a sweetheart who had decided to marry someone else, or when news of a wife's indiscretions reached him. He sent money orders back home, sometimes the sizable amounts accumulated by the great gamblers of the unit. In all these tasks, he was a model of prudence.

Now, he said simply, with the authority that the men's respect had conferred upon him, "I already know how the men feel. Everybody is pissed off, and they are waiting for somebody to do something."

I realized then that George had brought us together in the first place. He obviously had been talking to the men. With the help of some, he had handpicked us to lead. He had approached Shep, and Shep had recruited Shorty and me.

"That sounds hopeful," I said firmly. "We want to talk to all of them tonight. We have twenty-four guys to contact. Let's get to work."

None of us said a word to the other during the next day, but we received knowing nods of approval from other noncoms we encountered. One in particular, Jameson, smiled all day, obviously pleased that we were planning something.

When night had settled fully, we headed for the wet and windy bow again. Shorty began like a man dealing a hand of poker.

"All of the guys are aboard, except Jackson. That Uncle Tom son-of-a-bitch heard what I had to say and high-tailed for Captain Jarrett to tell him right away."

Jackson was the other master sergeant, a six-striper, who ran the motor shop. He was a competent mechanic, but I found him an unlikable loner who had no interest other than his own welfare. He was a small man, bright and nervous. He had reached a relatively high position not only by his competence but also by obsequious relationships with the officers. The men scorned him.

George reported, "All the men I spoke with said that it was fine with them. They all wanted to know what, when, and where, so they can join in."

Shep, confirmed in his expectations of support, reported proudly, "Just like I said, the men are with us. So what do we do now, Grillo?"

Despite the uneasiness in my stomach, I offered a plan that I believed would make our point but expose us to minimal retaliation. "Let's write a petition. Then, we'll ask the men to sign it. We'll send it to Colonel Leland. Each of us will play a visible role, so that we'll either win together or hang together."

My courage was building, as was that of the others. We knew that we were right and we were angry. No matter what the cost, we wanted the officers to know that we were angry.

"Whatever happens to one of us, happens to all of us, right?" Shep said.

We shook hands all around and began to choose assignments. I agreed to write the petition. George would take it around for signatures. Shorty would make the appointment to meet with the Colonel, and Shorty and Shep would deliver the document.

"What about Jackson?" Shep asked.

"Yeah, what about that Uncle-Tomming bastard?"

"Let's offer him the same opportunity to sign, and see what happens," I responded. With that, we closed our meeting on the bow deck. Scared but determined, I went immediately to my office and wrote and typed the petition.

I set forth our anger and humiliation at being billeted in the hold; the horrible conditions; the unfairness of having to shower in such awful water, especially when white troops had fresh water for showering; the indignity of being restricted to the narrow bow of the ship, without space to sit or lie down. The petition closed with the statement that these were all examples of discrimination, evidenced by the preferential treatment given to white troops. Our segregated condition underlay the insufferable injustices and indignities we faced.

Typing the petition on one sheet of paper, I made lines for signatures on a separate sheet, so we could keep them both in our possession. This was an idea I got from Jules, a Jewish soldier I had met when we were on a quiz show presented over our ship's radio. He had advised me that this strategy might help us avoid the appearance of a conspiracy.

By morning, the weather had cleared. The entire company was outside on the bow, enjoying the light breeze and the gentle, momentarily forgiving sea.

George took the petition and went from man to man, letting each read it and then sign the separate sheet. We could not have wanted a better emissary. Everyone trusted George.

All the men signed except Jackson. He was seen going to Captain Jarrett, presumably to keep the captain informed.

True to our commitment, we did little or no talking to one another. When all the signatures were gathered, we got our four-man group together for a brief chat. We agreed that it was time to seek an appointment with the colonel. Shorty and Shep took the petition and went searching for Captain Jarrett, through whom we would attempt to present the petition to Colonel Leland.

"How did it go?" I asked upon their return.

Shep replied, "Okay. Captain Jarrett just took it. He seemed to know what it was about, thanks to Jackson."

Then we went our separate ways. We were uncomfortable. and we did not want to talk. We stayed apart the entire day. What we set out to do was done. All that was left to do was to await the consequences.

Early in the evening, Captain Jarrett sent for me. He led me out onto the deck amidships and spoke earnestly to me. He was very different from Colonel Leland. "Are you sure you want to do this? You ought to think carefully before you take this step."

I replied, "I really appreciate your concern for us, but we are the objects of outrageous treatment. This is something we must do. We don't believe we can respect ourselves unless we do it."

"So you want me to give this to Colonel Leland?"

"Yes, sir."

"Okay," he said, and we walked back inside together.

Early the next morning I went to the headquarters room and busied myself with paperwork. The rest of the crew arrived slowly and just hung around anxiously.

Soon Captain Jarrett came in. In his Midwestern twang he told us, "Get all the noncoms together and have them here at ten o'clock. Colonel Leland wants to speak to you all."

We were apprehensive but not afraid. We were relieved that something was about to happen in response to all of our efforts of the past two days. We had spoken out, and this realization seemed to fortify us against any eventuality. As we crowded into the headquarters room, twenty-three of the twenty-four noncoms, we were silent and serious. Here and there someone would let out an anxious sigh. We looked at each other often, as though seeking support.

Promptly at ten o'clock Colonel Leland came into the room. He was a small man, small of body and small of mind. He was barely five and one-half feet tall. He could not have weighed more than one hundred and forty pounds. He had a small head and a thin face, his faint blonde mustache a complement to his piercing cool eyes. He was in all respects a miserable man: miserable in spirit, and miserable in the impression he made on others

We assumed that he had been given the command of black troops because he was a Southerner, and as such was deemed to know "how to handle black men." He spoke not with a drawl, but a sort of flat drone. The antithesis of a commanding presence, he was a short martinet, compensating for his sense of inferiority by being cold, aloof, and cruel. Every officer feared him, and they were always on edge when they were around him.

Without a word, Colonel Leland sat in the chair we had placed against the center of a bulkhead. Slowly he took the petition out of the inner pocket of his jacket. He reread it silently. Then he looked directly at me, knowing full well that I had written it. The hatred in his eyes evinced itself, and I returned the look with a passionate hatred myself.

Colonel Leland spoke in a dry, slow, and deliberate manner. "There has been no discrimination aboard this ship. All arrangements have been made in order to make the best of a difficult situation for all of us. Nothing has been done to favor one group of soldiers over the other."

He waited, as though expecting some response. No one spoke. The rage in our faces spoke for us, sitting there in silence.

After a few minutes, Colonel Leland arose and walked out of the room, looking to neither the right nor the left. Captain Jarred trailed him.

We did not gather for a *post mortem*. By now, the seriousness of our actions had sunk in. We did not need a reminder that silence was prudent.

We went about our routines for two or three days. Then, abruptly, some of us were ordered to move our gear to the outside second deck. The decks had been enclosed to make room for sleeping bunks. Finally! We had access to fresh air! We hoped to get other improvements. We looked forward to fresh water for showering; the itching caused by the sea water was extremely irritating.

But our hopes were not fulfilled. Within a week, we were sent back to the stench of the hold. White soldiers replaced us. We never knew what had spurred the delayed improvement, or what brought about its reversal. We were demoralized. We felt trapped and hopeless, and very much abandoned by the army. But we felt a great sense of accomplishment in having planned our protest and brought it to a conclusion. We did not plan any other protests while we were on the ship. Given the results of our first effort, we could not expect a more favorable response. On the contrary, we expected any further protest to provoke a more forceful response. We were thoroughly intimidated.

One matter we did settle, however: what to do about Sergeant Jackson. Without even any discussion about the matter, we subjected him to thorough ostracism.

No one sat next to him at meals. No one shared his tent once we were on land. I don't even remember where his tent was located. He was the most isolated person I have ever been around. Aside from work, all was silence and rejection. On occasion Jackson would forget himself and ask a question or make a statement. The men would move away without saying a word. So severe was our treatment of Jackson that I began to question the need for such cruelty.

After two solid years of this treatment, Jackson began to deteriorate—talking to himself, not sleeping, losing weight, signing up to see the doctor frequently. He even stopped coming to the mess tent, instead carrying his food to his tent, where he ate alone.

After observation, the officers ultimately decided that Jackson should receive a medical evaluation and be sent back to the States. He disappeared early one morning, taken by an officer to base headquarters and then flown back home. None of us saw him leave. He was simply whisked away, with no goodbyes or handshakes. Few words were spoken about him after he was gone.

The men also established a posture with which to confront the indifferent treatment our officers meted out to us. We assumed a reciprocal indifference, usually speaking only when spoken to and answering only specific questions, correctly and conscientiously but unsmilingly and uninterestedly. Only Captain Callan of "B" company managed to establish a certain rapport with his men that made for a an open, friendly relationship between soldiers and officers. Our indifference helped us to bear the disrespect and the disdain of our officers.

We believed that our officers feared us—and that they feared being perceived as soft if they were too friendly with us. There was absolutely no communication between us other than that required to do the work. We lived in separate worlds. We had no families to discuss, and no hopes to express, no beauties of nature to comment upon, no human or humane aspect to our interaction.

CHAPTER 15

On to India

THE VAST CONVOY of which our ship formed only a small part helped us to grasp the immensity of the war effort. We came to terms with the reality that it would be a long time before we saw American shores and our loved ones again. We knew that some of us would never make it back. Many did not, succumbing to malaria, typhus, amoebic dysentery, and the occasional fatal accident.

We were not trained for combat; our immediate mission foreclosed that possibility. So on the one hand, we realized that we would not face enemy fire, at least in the short term; on the other, we resented that we were not assessed as able, perhaps even potentially heroic, soldiers, competent and trusted to acquit ourselves well under fire. The prestige services, such as the Signal Corps, airplane maintenance, actually flying those beautiful planes, and the operation of the various supply depots, were all allocated to white units. We slogged in the seas of mud during the monsoons. Our job was building and maintaining roads and bridges.

We did not yet, however, even know our destination. We knew we were sailing south in the Atlantic, but to where?

"Where in Hell are they taking us?" asked Vincent.

"Well it's not to the Pacific because, if so, they'd take us through the Panama Canal," ventured Hugo.

"I'll bet we'll round the Cape of Good Hope, but God knows for what," guessed Cutty, correctly.

Hugo, pensively: "Wherever, it's a cinch that many of us won't make it back. Bye, bye, Jeanie!"

Cutty: "Just what I was thinking. Wonder when I'll see Martha again?"

Shorty: "There ain't a damn thing we can do about it but make the best of a bad thing."

Hugo: "Guess it's no action for a long time!"

Cutty: "No use even *thinking* about that."

So it went, for about an hour, with Hugo, Cutty, and Shorty, daydreaming about home and girls.

On or about the twentieth day we sighted South Africa. Slowly, as the ship approached shore, the outlines of a modern city began to emerge. The following day we landed at Durban, a bustling commercial and industrial city. Taxis, buses, and autos scurried about. Gleaming, tall buildings abounded. As we pulled into port, we saw a heavily engaged harbor and a clean, modern metropolis.

Just before we were let off the ship for a few hours of shore leave, Captain Jarrett crammed the entire company into a narrow space and read us a notice from the ship's commander: "Consorting with native peoples is an offense under South African law and will not be tolerated."

Then the captain added, in his twang, "I don't know what they mean by *consorting with native peoples.* Jes' don't consort wit' em."

I did not have the stomach for sightseeing. South Africa interested me not at all. I knew that it repressed blacks unmercifully. It seemed ironic to accept its hospitality en route to fight Hitler's racism. The insulting manner in which we were enjoined from contact with black South Africans intensified my disgust and anger. I also feared violating some rule of the oppressive country unwittingly.

We could visit with the East Indians, who occupied an uncertain niche between whites and blacks. I struck up a conversation with an East Indian merchant who sold newspapers—largely tabloids carrying lurid stories about celebrities. Plump, swarthy, and easy to meet, Rajid invited me to his apartment for dinner. I believe that he was drawn to me by my looks, for my combination of Spanish, African, and, perhaps, some residue of Carib Indian ancestries made me look like I could have been from India.

A large combination living and dining room gave notice that this family lived well. Rajid's wife, whom I met only for a second or two, presided over the home. She said not a word to me as, wrapped in billowing waves of silk, she dashed from kitchen to dining room bringing us little dishes of tasty fried delicacies, one of which I identified as lentils, and another as banana fritters.

At the first opening, Rajid asked me the question that I had anticipated: "How is it that you are in the American Army?"

"I was born in America, I am an American."

"But why are you with the blacks?"

"In America, anyone who has African blood is included in the black group, In many parts of the country, blacks and whites are kept separate by law."

"I know that our two nations have many similarities in social arrangements, but this is the first time I have seen it with my own eyes."

He explained South African *apartheid* to me, in which Indians represented a third racial group, with a restricted status. But they enjoyed some freedoms and opportunities not enjoyed by blacks.

Our conversation largely skirted the issues of South Africa's racial policies. We both had cagey and careful approaches, fearing possible retribution from whatever masters ruled us. He made it a point, however, to speak about the protest movements in which he participated, showing me posters and leaflets.

When it was time to board truck back to the ship, he accompanied me there. As we walked, he gave me a warm handshake, and said, "I am sorry we could not speak more freely."

Once the *Santa Paula* reached open sea again, we began to get an idea of our destination, for we sailed in a northerly direction in the Indian Ocean. We guessed North Africa or India, but we could not tell. India made no sense to us.

We stopped, but did not disembark, at Mombasa, Kenya, so we saw nothing of that land, for we were moored at sea. When we left Kenya, we sailed straight into the Indian Ocean, directly towards India.

In a matter of days we arrived at Karachi, our first encounter with the overwhelming millions of the Indian people. We were whisked through Karachi in new GMC trucks, through veritable seas of people draped in white. We rode for about two hours into the middle of the desert.

Recently built barracks, standing in total isolation, awaited us. Again the army had used its ingenuity to keep black and white soldiers apart. They placed us deep in the desert, in the middle of nowhere, where we could have contact with no one else. The explanation given for our isolation was that we were undergoing quarantine. That did not explain, however, why we had no contact with white soldiers, who must have been undergoing quarantine also.

We remained in the desert for almost three months. We spent long days doing nothing, and long cold nights singing bawdy songs, gambling, and drinking beer, when we had it. I was lucky, for I had my personnel work to keep me occupied. The Army keeps careful records; recording, recording, recording helped me to keep my balance and my sanity.

Finally we received orders to move out. Everything moved on our backs. First we loaded the train. Then we loaded and unloaded all the gear and equipment, from train to train to train to ferry to train again and then to trucks again, through the breadth of India, from Karachi in the northwest, to the farthest northeast, into the tea country of Assam, nestled against the Himalayas.

India's railroad tracks included a number of widths or gauges. Thus every time we reached a point in the journey where we encountered a different gauge, we had to transfer everything from one train to the other. It was steamy, back-breaking work in the hot India sun.

The trip across India took fifteen days. For all the discomfort, the mosquitoes, the searing heat, and the hard wooden seats, it was an adventure. Hour after hour we rolled through the countryside at a snail's pace—all that the trains were capable of, or a speed to which they were restricted for safety reasons.

Every time the train stopped, we ran out to the engine, swung the giant pipe that filled the locomotive with water out to the side of the train, pulled the chain that regulated the water flow, and drenched ourselves under it. Sometimes we were in our underwear, and sometimes we were fully clothed. It did not matter; we merely sought relief from the stifling heat.

The Indian countryside was one large belt of rich green grass. Over this vast expanse of land flew endless flocks of vultures, very large and very ugly, with naked red heads. We saw many group of the scavengers picking away at the carcasses of dead cows. They patrolled the fields like sentinels, swooping down unerringly upon even the smallest bit of carrion.

At night the darkness swallowed up the train, which now seemed tiny and inconsequential, as did its mission, when viewed from the perspective of the eons this land had existed and nurtured life. Keeping us company throughout the long nights, a myriad of fireflies added an almost mysterious luminosity to the eerie depths of silent darkness that now isolated us.

Though we did not have close contact with the Indian people, we saw them on the farms, working the land. They always gave us friendly waves as we passed by. At the ferry transshipment point we did come into close contact with large groups of commuting workers and families. They seemed largely to be poor. Only the petty entrepreneurs, selling their wares, appeared to enjoy a comfortable standard of living. We managed only the most casual talk with them, though many spoke English. We were obviously an unusual and strange sight to them, and they did not seem to know how to relate to us; or perhaps they were afraid to talk to us, for any number of reasons, for the atmosphere was palpably oppressive. We, reciprocally, were awkward in our attempts to converse. And we had neither the time nor the opportunity to interact at any length with the people, for we stopped but briefly at the way stations. So we did not get very far with each other.

At the end of our journey across India, we arrived at a tea plantation, a beautiful setting where we expected to stay for a while. The rich green leaves of the tea plants extended for acres. An ocean of growing tea surrounded us.

In the center of this oasis stood a tall steel and concrete structure, completely open on all sides. It was obviously a building related to tea production. Its floors were simple tiers of wire mesh placed about four feet apart in height, over which the green tea leaves were scattered to dry. A constant traffic of workers moved about the place, bringing in baskets of green tea leaves and taking out baskets of dried leaves. The light airy fragrance of tea blossoms permeated the atmosphere.

Our bunks rested on the ground cement floor of the building, from which the two bottom tiers of wire screening had been removed. Encircling the base of the building was an improvised wall of loosely woven wood lathes. This wall served as our only protection against the cold night air and against the unbearable heat during the days. We slept under two and three blankets in this refrigerator of a living space.

But we were not unhappy. The place was clean and dry. There were few insects to bother us. Despite the heat during the day and the harsh, cold nights, we adjusted to the rhythm of the climate and made ourselves comfortable. We looked forward to a lengthy stay, free from the noise, confusion, and the dangers of combat.

Both men and women carried the tea leaves in and out of the shed. We seldom saw adolescent girls, though boys worked alongside the adults. It soon became apparent that this strategy was deliberate: The adolescent girls wore no covering over their breasts. They were kept out of the shed, we assumed, to keep them out of our view. For they were all beautiful, their breasts full and firm.

Although they were tea pickers, they usually did not come close to the tea shed. On those few occasions when one did, all work stopped as we gathered to feast our eyes and lust over their beautiful dark bodies. We were starved for even the sight of women, so we seized every opportunity to enjoy the sensuality of these exposed, well-formed breasts.

"God damn!" sighed Shorty. "I never thought I'd see anything that beautiful again. Look at 'em, so firm and pretty. I sure would like to touch 'em."

"Touch 'em?" cried Valentine, almost in pain. "I'd give anything to bury my face in them and just lie there, kissing and nuzzling them. Man! They're beautiful!"

That was the extent of the contact with women that a few of us had. Only a relatively few men visited prostitutes on those rare occasions when we had access to them.

From this station, we maintained the airport from which flights with supplies were made over "The Hump," as the Himalaya Mountains were called, into China. I never saw the airport at Dinjan, the name of the village nearby. I was detached from my unit to serve as secretary to Colonel Henry T. Byroade. He seemed to be an important official on a diplomatic mission, serving as State Department liaison to the Chinese government, with whom the American government was cooperating on this operation.

A civil, cultivated man, Colonel Byroade drew high respect from all who dealt with him. He was urbane and easily correct in all that he did, and courtesy came as naturally to him as breathing.

I operated the teletype machine. He did not hesitate to ask my assistance in editing the copy he transmitted daily to New Delhi and Washington. In the course of the following years his name would appear in connection with high diplomatic assignments, including the ambassadorship to Korea.

The opportunity arose for me to become friendly with the staff of the Chinese office that was the counterpart of Colonel Byroade's operation. They took me twice to their luxurious apartment for elaborate meals: chickens lavishly cooked, vegetables in profusion, fruit for dessert. The conversation excited me no end. They perceived me as knowledgeable, yet had the courtesy not to attempt discussing any topic that could put me in a difficult position.

Colonel Byroade made a lasting impression upon me. He did no more than treat me as an intelligent, competent person, whose race and color were of no moment. He cared for me in the intangible ways human beings care for each other when stripped of words, gestures, and material exchanges of any type.

My idyll did not last. Abruptly, our unit was given orders to move to the Ledo Road, to build and maintain it. Colonel Byroade seemed truly regretful that I was leaving. His parting words to me aroused strong emotions in me: "You have been an enormous help to me. I shall miss you. I have admired your work very much. I certainly hope to see you when this is all over, and we shall be back in the states again. Meanwhile, God be with you."

We shook hands and parted. My heart was heavy. Sadness overwhelmed me. But I felt privileged to have known Colonel Byroade.

CHAPTER 16

The Ledo Road

WE WERE MOVED ABRUPTLY from our beautiful tea plantation. We drove directly into the jungle that formed a large part of the province of Assam. Our trucks lumbered through the little town that gave its name to the Ledo Road, the passage we carved through that beautiful but difficult country. We believed that the original trail that became the Ledo Road may have been cut by the Naga, a tribe that inhabited the area.

Short and stocky, the very strong Nagas had legs that reached nearly a foot in circumference at the calf. They walked the full thirty-four miles up and down the mountains two or three times a week, each time with supplies of food, such as rice and lentils, or pleated leaves, out of which they built their *bashas,* or living quarters.

The women did most of the carrying in baskets slung over their heads. Their legs were as powerful as the men's. The Naga lived high in the mountains. They never let us see the points at which they entered or left the trails leading to their small villages, deep in the jungle. Whenever we encountered a group, they were always already en route either down to the little town of Ledo or back to their clearings in the mountains. They lived deeper in the jungle and much higher than the camps we had established in flat country by the side of the Ledo Road.

Very adept at hiding the locations of their thatched huts, they never smiled or attempted any communication with us. But they presented no threat and did not make us feel uncomfortable in any way. Each carried a scimitar-like big knife, formidable to behold and very intimidating, until we became accustomed to viewing them as tools useful in hacking brush out of the way.

Once Sergeant Jim Wright, the ranking enlisted man in the medical detachment, found a trail. A tall, dark, handsome, and trim man, Jim exuded sharpness and always carried himself with an air of competence and confidence. He packed a small bag of medicines, mainly sulfa drugs, and anti-malarial drugs. He invited me to try to visit a Naga family in their habitat.

When we arrived at the hut, looks of suspicion greeted us. I feared our intentions would be misunderstood. But after much gesturing, we managed to convey that we had brought medicine. The patriarch favored us with the slightest smile, accepted the medicine, and let us know that he would be pleased when we left. We were on our way down the hill before the rest of the family emerged from the hut to take a curious look at us.

We pitched camp along a creek that made a slight clearing in the thick mass of vegetation. But as it turned out, we settled too close to its shores. This was monsoon country. We did not know yet about the heavy, constant soakings that eventually became a daily occurrence during monsoon season.

When we first entered the area that would become our home for twenty-four months, we encountered a family of about twelve gibbons, swinging high in the heavy growth of trees and tall bamboo that enveloped us. They did not jump from limb to limb or tree to tree; they *flowed,* so graceful and effortless were their movements.

They screeched loudly and excitedly, protesting our invasion. Their home—perhaps for centuries—abruptly taken away and destroyed, the gibbons gradually disappeared from sight, perhaps as punishment for our nerve and recklessness. They did not let us view any longer their beauty and eloquence of movement. We never saw another one.

The first sizable unit to reach the jungle, we arrived to build the first section of the Ledo Road and to improve and maintain that stretch. For month after boring, tedious month, literally engulfed by the jungle, we hacked out clearings in which to place our sleeping tents, to build latrines, and to locate the large headquarters tent, mess tent, supply tents, and other structures that sheltered us for more than two years.

Aided by gigantic bulldozers, earth movers, dumptrucks, and rock-crushing machines, we cut our way steadily alongside the mountains, ever creeping slowly higher until we reached the part of the road where another black labor unit, The 45th Engineer Regiment, was building the next section of the road. The 45th Regiment, much larger and more adequately equipped than our battalion, built a longer section of the road than we did, cutting it into northern Burma.

Precariously, we cut out of the side of the mountains a path barely wide enough for one truck to pass. Then we gouged additional land out of the mountain to make room for another lane of traffic and for the drainage ditch that accompanied the road along its course.

When we had finished removing the dirt and making the basic road, we covered it with tons of rock, crushed at the site, made from the boulders that surfaced as the earth was turned over. Packed and rolled so that it made a very hard surface, the road was neatly "crowned," so that rainwater could roll off it and into the drainage ditch dug on the inner boundary of the road.

Spectacular ravines formed the opposite boundary, the dreaded "open" side of the Big Snake, as some of us called the tortuously winding and treacherous road.

The ravines claimed many men in our unit while we built the road. Sometimes trucks or heavy equipment tumbled down the sides of the ravines—especially during the wet season—carrying the drivers and operators within them to horrifying deaths below. These accidents became less frequent as the months wore on and we were able to cut deeper and deeper into the mountains, thus making a wider and safer road.

Up, up the mountain we built, progressing slowly during the humid, hot days. As nature demanded, we had to build "horseshoe" curves, and "switchbacks" where the road coursed for miles northward and then turned to course for miles southward to the beginning of the horseshoe across the ravine. Endlessly, at the bottom of the horseshoes, the road would curve and turn north again, right or left, depending upon the direction of the vehicle, forming another horseshoe.

So, we began to straighten out the road by building bridges between the ends of the horseshoes, thus eliminating the miles and miles of road in-between that formed the horseshoe. Our engineer officers fancied themselves innovative and ingenious. They were cocky and strutted around, exercising their power with flair and flourish. They were good, but they had had no experience with such mountain jungle.

Our road work did not impress the Naga tribesmen, however. They stopped frequently to view our great feat of engineering. They seemed to be interested principally in the bridges, and would chatter among themselves excitedly about it.

Then it came! In sheets! The first monsoon of the season, twelve inches of rain in twenty-four hours—or was it twenty-four inches in twelve hours? Whatever the measurements, it was a deluge the likes of which none of us had ever experienced. In amazement, we watched our bridge swept away like so many matchsticks by the summer's accumulation of decaying bamboo, fallen trees, and other debris that had lain in wait at the base of ravine. This debris now accumulated against the bridge. Ultimately, the pressure of the debris, driven by torrents of water, overwhelmed the bridge and swept it away, so much debris itself.

We lost three men that morning. They had foolishly been assigned, by misguided and inexperienced officers, to stand on the bridge with long lengths of bamboo and push the onrushing debris under the bridge. The hope was to keep the water flowing and the accumulated debris from pressing against the bridge. It was a futile effort. The young soldiers became part of the debris itself, swept down the river like so many lengths of bamboo.

In the wake of the disaster, we understood the excited chatter of the Nagas as they watched us build the impossible bridge. They had foreseen the tragedy. Many times in the past they must have felt the power of a river, born overnight after an incredibly heavy rain, raging a destructive path towards the lowlands. Just as suddenly—returning the countryside to peace, the serenity, and beauty—the river receded, and the sun came out again.

During the transition from tea plantation to jungle, I had lost my post as personnel sergeant. I had been detached from the 823rd Battalion to work the temporary position as secretary and assistant to Colonel Byroade, but I still had my meals and recreation with the battalion.

When building the Ledo Road became the mission of the 823rd, however, there was no way I could stay with Colonel Byroade, for the Army had no provisions for detaching a black soldier to a neighboring white unit. I had to move out with the 823rd, however valuable my work with Colonel Byroade may have been.

I presented a dilemma to the officers. They may have been glad to get me out of the personnel sergeant's position, as it was a relatively influential post and I was perceived as a soldier who stirred things up. Trying to find a function for me, the adjutant asked me to take charge of the movie program. This was a signal that I would not be returned to the position of personnel sergeant. The move was viewed by the men as a reduction in my status. But I was pleased by the assignment, for it gave me great freedom, and responsibility only for myself, as long as I functioned effectively and posed no problems.

The job had been handled haphazardly because no single man previously had been responsible for the function. The movies would arrive irregularly on the mail-and-package truck that stopped at our unit daily. One member or the other of the headquarters staff would show the movie whenever one did arrive. Responsibility for the projector had also fallen to no one in particular. Frequently, no movie could be shown because the equipment was out of order.

Immediately, I began to catch a ride with Corporal George, our mail orderly, on those days when he had to drive to base headquarters to purchase money orders, mail packages for the men, or transact some other postal business. Thus enabled to procure and return the movies myself, and to get spare parts as soon as the projector needed any, I had assurance of a steady selection of movies and a dependable supply of parts for the machine.

The trip up and down the mountains was hot, very dusty on dry days, and very slippery on wet days. On wet days we drove very slowly, the vehicle winding carefully around the horseshoes, with ravines and disaster only four or five feet away. The tedious, dangerous journey took between two and one-half and three hours each way. During the wet season, it sometimes took as many as four hours one way.

I had a tent to myself from which to operate the movie program. This allowed me to store the projector and the movies properly, and to keep the projector in good operating condition. It was popular duty: Movies were extremely important to morale.

The men sat in the open on felled tree trunks that we had dragged to the area with bulldozers. When showing the movies, I protected the projector with an enclosure made of scrap canvas and wood strips.

One night we watched a movie that the men enjoyed very much despite a slow drizzle. By the next evening, however, a torrential rain was pouring on our campsite. I made preparations to settle down by my little hot stove, listen to the storm, and read a book or write letters.

Suddenly, a delegation of four or five men appeared at the entrance to my tent. I invited them in.

"Aren't we going to see a movie tonight?" asked Sergeant Valentine.

"We don't have another movie," I stammered.

"Oh, yes we do; we have the one that you showed last night. Can you show it again tonight?"

"Okay, but let's wait a while to see if the rain lets up a little."

"What difference does it make? We have to work in this damned stuff. We sure can take it while we watch a movie. Come on, Sarge. Get it on!"

His logic was unassailable. Besides, the men were in no mood to be denied one of the few pleasures remaining to them. I was a little worried that the heavy rain might damage the screen, but my better judgment told me to move into action, storm or no storm.

The entire company turned out, raincoats, rain hats, and rain boots on. The hilarity of the situation became apparent to all of us. So, in addition to enjoying an excellent movie again, we had a great time laughing at ourselves!

"What are you dumb bastards doing looking at a movie in a driving rain?" a nameless voice called out in the dark.

"The same thing you are doing, you stupid son-of-a-bitch!" came the anonymous reply. The screen survived.

Heavy rain was a constant during the monsoon season, and its effect upon the movie program was among the least of our concerns. The rains made a quagmire of the area, with mud deep enough to cover our calves, and sometimes our knees. Sometimes the unit was paralyzed. We were literally confined to our tents because we could not traverse even the short distance to the mess tent through a sea of mud. Our pathetic attempts to surround our tents with small drainage ditches quickly failed as the onrushing waters streamed through our tents.

One unpleasant distinction we resented keenly was that the officers' tents were all elevated—placed on platforms made of split bamboo—whereas the tents for enlisted men rested directly on the ground, sometimes on low ground at that.

The combination of the dreary, tedious, repetitive work and the long period we had spent at this miserable location began to have its effect on the men. Spirits began to sag alarmingly. The three horsemen of our own particular apocalypse were malaria, amoebic dysentery, and emotional breakdown.

Men would be seized suddenly by an attack of malaria. I had fourteen such attacks. But though malaria debilitated a sufferer to the point where he would wish to die, drugs such as atabrine and chloroquin could control it.

Amoebic dysentery presented a more serious matter. When it struck, a soldier's life was immediately threatened. Some men died from it.

Emotional disorders did not have the recognition they enjoy now. The result devastated the afflicted, since they were judged to be either malingering or simply "crazy." Some men would have extended bouts of depression, go on crying jags, or become belligerent and assault other soldiers.

The officers could not cope effectively with these situations. They would let a situation escalate into a crisis time after time. They could not develop mutually respectful relationships even with the large number of intelligent and educated men who belonged to our unit.

Instead they favored the so-called Uncle Toms, and the loudmouths, with whom they established a certain rapport. This, at times, made for a dangerous situation, wherein a particularly hostile soldier, now drunk, might threaten to spray the whole company with machine-gun fire, while his officer patron tried to settle him down.

No sanctions of any kind were ever imposed on the protected soldiers who broke out in rages. Threats of courts-martial were reserved for "smart niggers," like me, who became involved in discussions with officers about injustices and discrimination.

At one point, when I protested some utterly ridiculous order, an officer, Captain Jack Burl, threatened me with, "Sergeant, you know we have a guard-house for this kind of behavior."

I responded immediately, "I'm ready."

Captain Burl modulated his tone and modified his instructions. I believe he thereby avoided arousing others who looked to me for leadership.

We did not have the drama, the crushing misery, of battle; there was never a mass loss of life in combat. Twice we were bombed by the Japanese, fortunately with no injuries or deaths resulting. Our main defenders were British and Indian units, which manned anti-aircraft artillery. Occasionally, antiaircraft fire would strike a Japanese bomber that exploded instantly into a million bits, like a gigantic matchstick being struck across the sky—a spectacular, macabre sight.

We all had to take cover in slit trenches we had dug in anticipation of such an attack. My partner in the slit trench was Joe Greene, the most successful gambler in our unit. He had the devil-may-care attitude of a seasoned tough *hombre*. He stored his hundred-rupee notes, each worth thirty U.S. dollars, loosely in a cigar box, and never hid the box, even while he slept. The men were all convinced that tampering with Joe's rupees would invite sure, swift, and violent retribution.

In the slit trench, though, we were simply two scared soldiers as we witnessed the drama of the Japanese bombers unfolding above us. Breathing deeply, Joe asked me, "Sarge, are you scared?"

Trembling and breathing as deeply, I replied, "I'm scared shitless, Joe." We sat silently with an occasional grunt throughout the hour or so before the all-clear sounded.

One of our men operated a machine-gun emplacement during the brief attacks. A mad rush took place on the part of the officers to present the soldier with a Silver Star, the only combat decoration awarded a soldier in our unit while in India, in an obvious and desperate effort by our battalion commander to receive combat recognition.

We were isolated and insulated. China separated us from Japan and the Pacific theater of the Far East. India separated us from the action in the Soviet Union, North Africa, and Europe. The China-Burma-India (or CBI) Theater was like a sideshow of World War II. The expectation seemed to have been that CBI would emerge as a major theater of action. That did not happen.

CBI, nonetheless, represented a major commitment of Allied men and materiel. We stayed mostly in a readiness mode, waiting for an anticipated land war in Burma that never came to pass.

Mindful of our relative safety from the brutalities of combat, we knew that, except for a very few of us, our lot was not nearly as bad as that suffered by say, combat infantrymen in Europe, or sailors sunk in battle in the Pacific. By the time we opened a land route into Burma, so that U.S. forces could engage the Japanese directly, World War II was nearing its end.

A U.S. buildup on the Burma border began just months before the war drew to a close in Germany and Japan, as it turned out. We had opened the land route to Burma, presumably to connect to the Burma Road and thus have a way for men and materiel to be transported into China. Truck convoy after truck convoy roared over the road we had built, carrying supplies, equipment, and men for what was now a "real" war. A unit of highly trained and touted infantrymen, Merrill's Marauders, arrived and went into Burma to engage the Japanese, only to be decimated pathetically by "mite" typhus, a fever spread by a practically invisible parasite. We met the members of this highly touted group in the hospitals, the only unsegregated facilities in the army. They died by the dozens, their uniforms and gear piled high outside the hospital. I believe that the medical professionals finally used air-conditioned wards to help the men bear the blazing fevers to which "mite" typhus made them subject. But a large number died before that relief came.

Despite our escape from the rigors of combat, we had our own desperations to contend with, and they were real to us: the constant heavy rain during the wet season, the ever-present choking dust during the dry season, the mud in which we wallowed much of the time. The fact that for thirty-two months we were out of contact with any women—except army nurses when we became ill—served to make us even more tense and unhappy. The closest we ever came to having Rest & Relaxation was during two trips wherein the entire battalion was taken to Calcutta. We had to repeat the madness of tran-shipping all the equipment from the narrow-gauge railroad to the wide-gauge and back again, transferring the entire battalion's cooking, eating, and sleeping equipment every time the tracks changed width.

Our lack of leave time was racism so blatant, so discriminatory, that we could not talk about it without fuming. In one discussion we reviewed the facts carefully, so that there could be no question about them if ever we got the opportunity to lodge a protest. These disgruntled men were all intelligent and well-educated soldiers, who carried major responsibilities within the unit. Charles, the youngest and the brightest, stated the issue succinctly: "Fur-loughs are given to white soldiers on an individual basis. They can travel to any place within India that is on an approved list. We are not even told about opportunities such as the chance to see the Kashmir—described in all the literature as ethereally beautiful—or to visit the Taj Mahal, 'India's Jewel,' known the world over as one of the planet's most beautiful man-made works. Black soldiers have no such individual choices. We are forced to travel primitively, in one large group, almost as though we are prisoners. Come to think of it, that's not far from the truth, for black soldiers: We are treated like prisoners."

During one trip, we had been taken to a riverbank near Calcutta, where tents had been pitched to accommodate us, with only primitive arrangements for toilets, and with all our meals cooked and served field-style—exactly what we were supposed to be resting and relaxing from.

We were even situated close to the burning *ghats,* the rivershore platforms on which India cremates its dead on piles of wood.

As circumstance would have it, during our stay in India horrible famines assailed that country. So the sights included a steady stream of dead bodies floating past our campsite, a sight which left us literally ill with disgust.

The great obscenity of Calcutta was the dead bodies. They would lie on sidewalks waiting for the trucks that circled the city constantly, picking up the bodies unceremoniously and pitching them atop the bodies already loaded. Walking down the sidewalk, we had to cross from one side of the street to the other and back to avoid dead bodies. The experience of Calcutta made the return to the jungle welcome.

We did not see any other black troops in Calcutta. We were curiosities to the Indian people. Neither did we see many white soldiers; we assumed they were holed up in hotels and restaurants. Mostly we wandered the streets and went into the shops for endless bargaining sessions with merchants. They practically held us hostage until we bought something, never letting us leave until they offered a price that we would accept. It was obvious that the markup was still enormous.

Too afraid and disgusted to roam the streets of Calcutta after dark, the men would all return to the compound in early evening. The talk then was of those dead bodies and what it did to us to walk among them. Shep McCants had tears in his eyes when he said, "I just can't take it any more. I simply won't go back into those streets again."

We turned our attention over the next few days to getting back to the jungle, and all of the sweat and hard work that the return journey would entail. The jungle seemed hospitable when compared to Calcutta.

After our last "vacation" in Calcutta, our outlook turned to rage. We were testy and churlish. I believe our officers began to fear us.

CHAPTER 17

Give Me Some Men

INTO THIS PHYSICAL AND EMOTIONAL MORASS entered the most memorable person I met in the army. To our surprise and delight, Captain Robert Penn, the only black commissioned officer we saw during our thirty-two month stay in India, joined our unit as chaplain. Good fortune brought him to us.

Excitement ran throughout the compound like a brush fire. When we finally saw the captain close up, and could talk to him, we greeted him with great enthusiasm. "Welcome, welcome, welcome," one soldier repeated. "Man, we've needed you for a long time," another added, expressing the entire company's relief that finally we had a black officer with us. "Let us know what we can do to make you comfortable," was heard from every side. Men smiled extravagantly and held on for seconds longer than usual when shaking his hand for the first time.

Captain Penn's charisma and sincerity charmed us out of our shoes. About five feet nine, trim, obviously fit, he looked like an ex-athlete in his early forties who still maintained his training routine. Not an extra ounce of weight marred the impression he projected of strength—physical, mental, and emotional. His smile was constant and genuine. His brow furrowed when he listened intently to a soldier. He moved softly among us, shaking one hand after another, his solid muscular arm fairly bursting through his khaki shirt sleeve. "And where are you from?" he would ask a soldier, in a well modulated, pleasantly even voice—not deep, but not light either. The greeting was a prelude to the brief discussion he had with every soldier he met. He let us know immediately that he was very approachable. His manner communicated that he was there to serve us, to be with us, to live among us, to share fully "the black man's burden" that was our lot.

While we were punctilious in our treatment of him, referring to him always as "Captain Penn," he took, and we gave him, the liberty of calling us by the nicknames we called one another as soon as the necessary comfort level was established between us.

"The colonel has done something right for a change," shouted Ollie Wright, our supply sergeant. "Man, who could have thought of it," echoed Hugo Brooks and Oscar Hanes.

Powerful and confusing emotions welled up within us, and two little silver bars pinned on the collar of a black man were all it had taken to unleash them. We remembered well all of the many affronts to our dignity we had taken. Now here stood this approachable human being, witty, intelligent, unpretentious, representing the best in each of us. We, who had not seen a black officer for almost three years, felt the arrival of this immaculately uniformed chaplain was a gift, a gift from God. We even wanted to touch Captain Penn; he was the only human being we had had to touch with love since we left the States almost three years earlier. He gave himself to us to be respected, admired, and loved. And he generated profound and pleasant feelings within us in return.

"Hello, Sergeant Roberts. That's an impressive string of stripes. What do you do?" Shorty, so proud he had difficulty containing himself, explained his duties as sergeant-major and added, "Whatever we can do to help you get settled, just let us know. We'll have a crew of men ready to assist you. There isn't a man among us who wouldn't volunteer for that assignment!"

"Where are you from?" he asked Sergeant Wright. They found a common root in Tennessee, and they spent five minutes exploring it, with a burst of laughter when they recalled something happy and funny. "Where in the States did your outfit train? How long did the trip across the ocean take? What was South Africa like? Did you find it interesting? Were you able to see and do anything? What do you do for recreation?" The questions came in a steady stream. He was a good listener, intensely absorbing what any soldier described. He spent a good two hours with us in this initial encounter.

He had his tent located next to the headquarters tent, to provide easy access to the men. Housed in a double tent, he used one side for sleeping, the other for pastoral work. We spent evening after evening in bull-sessions in the captain's tent.

Many such sessions were dedicated to events back in the States. In others, we would recount experiences we had in common. Sometimes we talked about our work, or about India. The agenda became whatever caught the attention and interest of the group. Largely, the comfort of being with the captain, and the joy of the fellowship that he stimulated, attracted us.

He asked the men to build a chapel. They built him a cathedral out of the trees that abounded around us. The structure that the men built doubled as a theatre large enough to accommodate our movies and the USO shows that visited our compound.

Built out of logs from the tallest trees to be found in the jungle, the chapel was seventy-five feet long and thirty-five feet wide. It had a properly pitched roof so that the water ran off easily during a rainstorm. Over the roof frame, the men laid large pieces of heavy salvage canvasses, such as came from wrecked or otherwise inoperable trucks. Open on all sides, it protected us only from rains that fell directly down. We had a small problem with winds blowing the rain from the sides, but our rain gear kept us comfortable enough in a storm. The stage was made of very rough-hewn lumber, salvaged from large packing cases in which heavy equipment arrived. For seats we dragged in short lengths of wide-diameter trees and sawed out a V-shape from each; with further trimming, they made adequate seats with backs. There it stood, our magnificent cathedral.

Things began to happen rapidly after Captain Penn came. One day he gave me a set of keys to a jeep—the colonel's jeep, no less. Even the colonel had been caught up in our enthusiastic response to the chaplain. To his credit, he bought into the chaplain's program. "Here, Grillo [*the men couldn't handle my first name*]—you are now my assistant for recreation and morale. The job is yours to be what you want it to be." Captain Penn gave me the details of his conversation with Colonel Leland. The colonel had asked Captain Penn to assume the function of Recreation and Morale Officer. Captain Penn had replied:

"On one condition."

"What is that?"

"I will take on the function if I can pick my assistant and if he is provided with his own transportation."

"Whom are you thinking about?"

"Sergeant Grillo," Captain Penn had replied. "So, here we are," he said.

"We could not have got a better man," he continued. "Unless you feel the need to discuss something with me, you can go right to it and do what you think is necessary and possible. Just keep me posted from time to time and tell me where to sign for what you need."

All this good news surprised and pleased me greatly. "Gee, what a lucky break for me. I love what I am doing. Now, with your help, I can do so much more. Goodness knows the men need it. We are walking around like zombies. How'd you pull it off?"

"It was easy. The colonel approached me, so I was in the driver's seat. Besides, I had the right candidate. Although uncomfortable with your militancy, the officers know that you are a competent and resourceful man, and a hard worker. What's more, the colonel knows that you are a man of integrity, and that you won't use your freedom, and the jeep, improperly. We didn't even discuss that. You have earned the position; the men respect you highly and have come to expect this contribution from you. They will be delighted by your selection, and would have been disappointed if any one else but you got the position." His face beamed with the pleasure of the moment. "I think we're going to have fun. Now, let's get to work."

For the first time I had gotten a positive reflection from Colonel Leland. I very much appreciated the fact that Colonel Leland solved the matter of transportation so simply and directly. In a sense, the jeep symbolized respect and let the men know that he was thinking of them, too.

The next morning, I struck out early for base headquarters, where I had been negotiating with the Recreation Officer for some instruments for a volunteer jazz band we were organizing: drums, a saxophone, a trumpet, guitars, a trombone. When I returned that evening with as many instruments as I could get into the jeep, it was like Christmas.

Steadily Captain Penn and I arranged for other amenities for the men. Some time before Captain Penn joined us, I had the unit's powerful radio receiver located in my tent so that we could use the regular news reports to publish a one-page newsletter that carried news of the war. On the hour, we would hear broadcasts from New Delhi, Moscow, London, and the Armed Forces Radio Network. Sergeant James Valentine (who had taken my place as personnel sergeant), Corporal Brooks, and any other member of the headquarters staff member available came daily to the tent in the morning. They took longhand notes from the broadcasts, checked with one another to make sure that they had the correct information, wrote the stories, and typed and mimeographed *The Hairy Ears Herald*—named after the slang term for engineers.

The Hairy Ears Herald became a hot item for miles along the road. The soldiers preferred it to the official newspaper, which was not a daily and did not carry ongoing news of the war. Instead, it relied to a great extent on feature stories of little interest to the men. Worse yet, it came at irregular intervals, so that it was not reliable. It was called the *CBI Times* or some similar name.

At one point, the staff of the *CBI Times* had been ignorant enough to print a stereotype cartoon of a bulldozer-driving black soldier, complete with vastly exaggerated lips. We did not react too strongly; it seemed useless, and by now we were inured. But it was one of the reasons why we had no interest in the official newspaper.

The Hairy Ears Herald carried only the facts: so many German divisions destroyed by the Russians, so many Japanese planes brought down, a major sea battle won, another island captured, the Luftwaffe defeated over England, and the like. Not one "cute" feature story was carried. The news was what mattered to the men; it spoke directly to the question of if, and when, we would someday go home.

Soldiers from white units stationed along the same stretch of road came daily with reams of mimeograph paper to exchange for copies of the newsletter. *The Hairy Ears Herald* became a public-relations vehicle of great value for our unit. The personnel at Base Headquarters, very aware of our operation, began to use our cathedral as the center for entertainment in our area.

Our location became a stop for USO shows. It was the only facility that offered protection from rain during the wet season. The interaction with the entertainers gave the men great pleasure. Base Headquarters even provided us with a piano, which remained on our stage permanently. Soldiers from a ten-mile radius came to see the movies and the shows, including one show in which movie actor Pat O'Brien (star of 1940's *Knute Rockne, All American* with Ronald Reagan) and model-actress Jinx Falkenberg (of *Two Latins from Manhattan* and *Two Señoritas from Chicago*) jammed with us until three o'clock in the morning.

Next, we built a night-lighted basketball court. We marked out a regulation-size court in the dirt and passed a heavy roller over it until the dirt was nearly as hard as clay. We needed a good supply of 250-watt light bulbs to light the court, since in the coolness of the night, one or two of the bulbs would always burst immediately when the generator was turned off.

During one of our so-called vacations in Calcutta, I visited the actor Melvyn Douglas (of *Ninotchka* fame), who was now the Special Services Officer for the entire China-Burma-India Theater of Operations. He listened in fascination to my story of a lighted basketball court in the jungle. More importantly, he understood fully the worth and the need. From then on I received a biweekly a box of one dozen 250-watt light bulbs, which I supplemented with purchases in the little town of Dibrugarh, about thirty-five miles away.

The basketball program prospered hugely. The units in our vicinity formed a league of eight teams. The league games featured a number of players who had enjoyed outstanding college careers. Occasionally, crowds of two thousand came from miles around to watch the championship games. The units represented were all service units, that is, noncombatants: signal corps, quartermaster, ordnance, and the like. They had been, like us, in the jungle for months on end, waiting for the day, which never came, when we would be in direct combat with Japanese forces in large numbers.

The basketball league became the center of interest and entertainment for the troops in the area for almost a year. The court was booked nightly, except for an occasional USO show and the regular movies. For the first time black and white troops were integrated in one program in India. As fate would have it, the championship game, a game of very high quality, was played between two white teams, quite evenly matched, each having a college all-star or two on its roster. The game was the talk of the Ledo Road for two or three days before hand. The night of the game itself was electric. A large crowd came from throughout the base. Our company had prepared the court well, keeping it watered so that the dirt would remain packed and solid. The game superbly played, the score remained close until the very end, when the best player bagged a long arch for the final points. Just another good American basketball game. Afterwards, the teams and fans lingered and socialized, still enjoying the excitement that the game had generated. For a few moments we were oblivious to the gulf that usually separated white from black, especially in the army, the protector of all our freedoms.

CHAPTER 18

Almost

IN THE SPRING OF 1944, Colonel Leland returned to the States. Major Richard Broulliere, who hailed from Wisconsin, replaced him. Major Broulliere arrived without fanfare such as greeted Captain Penn. He walked slowly through the compound, saying a soft hello to the few soldiers that he met.

A very large, full-muscled man, he could easily have been a powerful lineman on his college football team. Perfectly erect, he stood three inches taller than anyone else in the compound. He had a permanent quiet smile on his face. He spoke softy, just loudly enough so he could be heard clearly. His soft voice, and his deference to anyone with whom he spoke, proved that he did not need the outward trappings of power. He was powerful. His character made him so. He seemed to get much of his information by simple observation rather than interrogation. He conveyed, without speeches or gestures, his respect and regard for his men.

On this first tour he seemed interested in the condition of the camp.

"How long have you lived in that tent, soldier?" he asked.

"Two years," came the plaintive reply.

"Do you have much trouble with rats?"

Rats were the bane of our existence, climbing all over our mosquito netting. We used the netting to keep the rats off as much as the mosquitoes away. Major Broulliere took an especially long look at the creek, whose banks needed weeding and which was cluttered by debris scattered here and there.

Upon his return to headquarters, he immediately began to make changes that showed his care. His first contribution was to redo the compound completely. He got rid of the old tents—the ugly, hot, rotting canvas American tents—and replaced them with British tents, which were much better suited to tropical climates. Made of very heavy waterproofed cloth, not canvas, each had a double top, with a large air space between the tops for insulation. They were half-again larger and infinitely more comfortable than the American tents.

And then, wonder of wonders, Major Broulliere had the men's tents elevated off the ground on platforms of bamboo, just as the officers' tents had been from the very beginning of our jungle stay.

He had the underbrush cleared completely away, so rats would have no place to breed. He had the creek completely cleaned out to better control flooding during the wet season. Within three months he had our jungle abode, once a heavily overgrown patch of vines, plants, and bushes, clear and neat and infinitely more suitable for living.

Soon after his arrival, Major Broulliere called Captain Penn in and asked him to describe my work. Shortly after that conversation, a concrete-floored double tent arose in the front of the compound solely for my work. For the first time I had ample room in which to work and to store all of the recreation supplies I had accumulated: basketballs, nets and hoops, footballs, musical instruments, baseballs, mitts, bats, lights, a motion-picture projector, spare parts, screens, paints, games, books, cards, and ping pong equipment.

Most importantly, I had a proper setting in which to publish *The Hairy Ears Herald,* now well established throughout the entire region. I had a mimeograph machine exclusively for the newsletter, the radio, a large table, and space to store the reams of paper that neighboring units provided. After this, it became easier for Captain Penn and me to arrange amenities for the men.

Major Broulliere did this without fanfare, and with little conversation with me. He spoke with Captain Penn, and simply ordered that those who had or could procure resources, do so. For me, he had an ever-present smile and a hearty, "Hi, Sergeant! How goes it?" This was never an invitation to chat. Major Broulliere was not chatty. But he made my life as pleasant as it could have been at the time.

This situation did not last long, for the war was now clearly approaching its end. Every day the news generated greater optimism. This was the summer of 1944, and the Allies were at last getting the upper hand in the war against the Axis powers. Though we did not anticipate the rapidity of the end, we became very hopeful that our jungle saga would be over soon.

It was not over, however, before we had one final dramatic night—one which highlighted, a month before I left India, how harrowing and demeaning our experience as black troops had been. Sergeant Bender saw to that.

Sergeant Bender, the first sergeant of Headquarters Company, got his appointment, it seemed to me, because of his lack of identification with the men and his obsequious behavior toward the officers. He was insecure, gruff, insulting, and obscene.

He didn't have a single friend in the unit, though his ostracism was not nearly as severe as that we had provided for Sergeant Jackson earlier. With the good news coming from everywhere about the progress of the war, a celebratory mood descended on the camp. The members of the band came up with the idea of having a party to honor the mess sergeant, Sergeant James, on his birthday. Sergeant James had struggled heroically day in and day out with the task of providing the men three appealing meals with the limited ingredients available: the hated SPAM, canned vegetables, powdered eggs, freeze-dried potatoes, rice, and beans.

But he managed to conjure up interesting ways to prepare the food. He crushed the SPAM and seasoned it highly, and used onions, pimentos, and pickles for color and taste. He thereby produced a dish that made an excellent sandwich spread. He cooked the rice always to perfection, each grain separated, and his red beans reminded us of Louisiana.

His spirit, however, nurtured us as much as did the food. He was always busy planning three or four meals ahead. He always had a cake for special days. Not the stereotype of a jolly, plump cook, he was a professional. The troops considered him an enormously resourceful hero. He took his training at Army Cooks School seriously. In addition, he had undergone some training before entering the army. He knew he was competent, and he treated himself with the same great respect he offered us. He made friends of all of us; not bosom buddies, just good friends. He was intelligent, articulate, and sensitive. We liked to listen to him as he talked out his plans for a future meal:

"We're going to do something different with those canned string beans this time. I am going to pour the water off. We'll be losing some nutritional value, but the men don't like the taste of the water and they won't eat the beans anyhow. Then I'll lightly salt and pepper them and add a taste of curry. I'll add some tomatoes and cover this all with sliced onions, which I'll let wilt over the beans. Served over rice. I think the men will like that."

We saved our beer ration secretly. We bought every live chicken at the bazaar in Ledo. We enlisted the kitchen crew in the plot, and we made the sergeant take the day off.

Zollie Wright, the supply sergeant, provided a large tent for the bash. We strung lights, and streamers that we had purchased at the bazaar. We made the place look as cheery as we could. Then, we brought our beer and dumped it into the large cans that Sergeant Wright had provided, again using ice purchased in Ledo. The instruments, tuned and ready, pointed to a good time.

Then we brought Sergeant James to his party, a jam session in his honor. The band played, as the occasion inspired, at its very best: *groovy,* we termed it in our day, or *cool,* in today's vernacular.

This was a special occasion for the band, for they were honoring Sergeant James. They gave it all they had, sweating profusely, while stomping and shaking wildly to the music. We danced joyfully, with total abandon, inside the tent and out, improvising all manner of solo dances. At one point we formed a circle, and each soldier did his number. Some were excellent displays of talent: tap, soft shoe, buck. Some had good voices, belting out blues and ballads with great style and feeling. Others who had little talent improvised and gyrated and jumped.

Throughout the party we reached into the large cans for a beer or grabbed a piece of fried chicken. But no one got very drunk. Somehow, we all behaved well. It was a good party. No one wanted to mess up the most fun we had ever had in the jungle.

Jason, whose talents we did not know about, sang several ballads beautifully, sounding something like Ray Charles (many years later) singing "I Can't Stop Loving You." Clifford, the band's vocalist, belted out several gutsy blues numbers.

Occasionally, the entire group would burst into song, especially on well known songs like "Sunny Side Of The Street" or "Pretend." We clowned and laughed at each other uproariously. We hugged each other over and over again. I believe that somehow we had an idea that we were nearing the end of our time together. While we anticipated the joy of going home, there was a certain nostalgia as we also anticipated the separation from one another that the end of the war portended. There was a certain urgency to the hugs, as though we knew this was the only chance we would have to hug each other this openly and this emotionally before separating, probably never to see one another again.

Into this joyous chaos burst Sergeant Bender, precisely at ten o'clock, the curfew hour, and shouted, "Okay, cut this out!"

We stood there in stunned, angry silence. No words would have been appropriate with the impossible Sergeant Bender. As soon as he turned and went out of the tent, however, Sergeant Oscar Haynes played the opening bars of "Take The A Train" on his saxophone. We were off and running again.

Thirty minutes later, Sergeant Bender returned, this time accompanied by Lieutenant Simmons, the company commander. The lieutenant asked in a soft voice—he was not seen as a bad guy: "What's going on here?"

Too angry to consider the consequences, I immediately stepped forward and said, "Lieutenant, I have disobeyed an order. You should know that if I am given that order again, under the same circumstances, in the same manner, by the same person, I will disobey it again."

I was angry, very angry. The men were angry and disheartened. The lieutenant then said, "Well, break it up. We'll deal with this in the morning."

Pandemonium broke out after the two left. The men were furious. Their eyes were all red and wet with anger. Immediately some men went looking for hand grenades to throw into Sergeant Bender's tent. The entire compound was literally in an uproar. Cries of "Let's kill him" came from several tents. Mutinies are not realized until something dramatic happens, but as I saw it, we had a potential mutiny on our hands. We gathered in tents talking about what had happened.

"Killing is too good for the bastard," screamed one soldier.

"We weren't hurting anyone," yelled another.

"Why should that asshole be the first sergeant in the first place?"

"Because he's an Uncle-Tomming son-of-a-bitch, that's why."

The arguing went on for a full two hours, with the cool heads trying to restrain the hotter ones. I was among those trying to dissuade the group that was intent on fragging Sergeant Bender. Their plan was more than idle talk.

Finally, Big John—the tallest, most muscular, and clearly one of the toughest of all the men, and a great gambler—stood up and walked over to a soldier brandishing a hand grenade. He snatched it out of the soldier's hands. Then he spoke:

"All right, you crazy motherfuckers, the Sarge here has been with us all the way from MacDill Field, and he's never let us down. Now he's telling us we should be cool and go to bed. Well, I am going to take his advice! Anybody who wants to keep this shit going any further can expect to get his ass whipped by me personally."

That did the trick. The compound turned slowly to order. The men stayed up discussing the incident, but slowly they drifted off to bed, some quietly weeping in anger and frustration. Finally, at about two o'clock, all was quiet. I went to my own tent, exhausted, frustrated, and angry beyond sanity, yet relieved that we had averted violence.

The next morning I slept through breakfast. I awoke, washed my face, and started for the kitchen, where my breakfast would always be saved. Then I headed for the recreation tent. I was stopped by Corporal George. He told me, "The men all know that the major has sent for you. I have a message for you.

The men told me to tell you that whatever happened to you was going to happen to all of us. Don't be afraid, we mean to see that nothing happens to you."

Sure enough, as I entered the recreation tent, Shorty Roberts, the sergeant-major, met me and announced, "The major wants you to come to his tent right away." Then as an aside, he said, "Steady, everything is going to be okay, or there'll be Hell to pay."

Confused feelings welled up inside of me. I approached Major Broulliere's tent. He gave me a hearty handshake and greeting. Then he asked me, "What happened last night, Sergeant?"

"I'll repeat it to you, just as I said it to Lieutenant Simmons last night. I disobeyed an order. If I am given that order again by Sergeant Bender, I shall disobey it again. I am ready to accept whatever happens to me."

I summarized the incident, then explained what had happened afterward as well:

"After the lieutenant and the sergeant left, the men milled about angrily. Some of the men wanted to throw a live hand grenade into Sergeant Bender's tent. Some men—particularly Private Williams—helped me to quiet the others. Finally, we got them all into bed. But the angry talk continued until about three."

Colonel Broulliere did not say a word for a long time. His face was somber, and he shook his head slowly from side to side in what appeared to be disbelief. He seemed disgusted, and though I trusted him I wondered if some of his disgust had to do with my behavior.

Soon he began: "Sergeant, when I heard the music and the singing last night, I wondered how men who have been in this God-forsaken jungle over two years could still have it in them to play music, to sing, and to laugh as happily as you were laughing. I admired the men very much. I was proud of my troops. You, I respect especially, for I know what you have done. You were nothing short of heroic and I am personally appreciative for what you did in averting violence. You go back to the compound and do exactly what you have been doing. I appreciate it deeply."

Tears welled in my eyes as I heard these kind, warm words from the major. I saluted smartly, said a crisp, soldierly, "Yes sir"—the crispest one I had ever given during my entire army career—did a snappy about-face, and walked briskly and proudly away.

Several of the men who worked around the compound gathered with Captain Penn in his tent to await my return from the visit to Major Broulliere. I told them that everything was fine, that the Major had treated me very well.

"Attaboy, Gandhi! [*This was a nickname Shorty had given me.*] That's the way it oughta be," he shouted. "Not everyone is stupid. We have a man for a commanding officer now!" Captain Penn gave me a tight hug, saying very little, but keeping his eyes on me.

"Why don't you take the rest of the day off and rest," Shorty suggested. "We'll take care of business for you. There's no game or movie tonight, so you can take it easy."

I took Shorty's advice and went to my tent. Throughout the day men came by my tent to congratulate me and to talk about the previous evening.

Meanwhile, Major Broulliere had been busy. He summarily removed Sergeant Bender from the post of first sergeant and ordered him to move across the road, away from the men. He immediately began the arrangements to send Sergeant Bender back to the States. Lieutenant Simmons, I believe, was transferred from his post to a lower, subordinate position in another company, as a line officer.

I was treated like a hero. It was a rich and fulfilling experience, and the high point of my army career. This black Cuban had done all right as a black American leader of men, and I was proud.

I was returned to the States within a month, in January 1945, by plane. I stopped in Iran, Persia, Egypt (where I saw the Pyramids and the Sphinx), Senegal, and at Natal, Brazil.

Upon arriving in the States I marked time until my discharge, in September of 1945. I did not participate with any enthusiasm in the celebrations of victory over Germany in the spring, and over Japan in late summer. I don't even remember where I was on either occasion. I was still too drained by my experiences in the jungle in India.

I had earned my little victory in India, in the jungle, where I won one small battle in our private war against the most immediate enemy black soldiers faced in World War II, the status quo in the United States Army.

Epilogue

IN EARLY 1949, after three years of graduate study in Latin American History at Columbia University, I decided to move to California. It was one of the best decisions of my life. I took a post as director of the Alexander Community Center, a part of the recreation department of the City of Oakland.

I had formed a vague notion of putting my uncommon background to good use by serving as a link between black and Spanish-speaking people, and in Oakland I found myself in the middle of a mix of Mexican-Americans and black Americans living in one of the poorest neighborhoods of a thriving city. These two communities formed the vast majority of the Alexander Community Center's clientele. Both groups were generally held in low esteem by the whites of Oakland, and in this neighborhood they shared all the public institutions for education, recreation, social welfare, and health, as well as probation and parole facilities.

My two years at the center were among the happiest I have known. The counselor who had helped me find the position observed, "The Oakland Recreation Department has a superb in-service education program." They did, and even my high expectations were exceeded. It was just what an eager, cocksure young man needed. It opened up to me a world of understanding that I still sorely lacked.

During those two years, I attended weekly seminars, offered to the Recreation Department's professional staff, under the leadership of Dr. Gertrude Wilson, author of the important study *Social Group Work*. A professor at the University of California-Berkeley's School of Social Welfare, she offered a first-rate, graduate-level introduction to the field.

I became a sponge, absorbing insights and knowledge far beyond the self-centered, assumed competence of a young man not so long out of school and the military. I began to give more attention and respect to the different cultures, social attributes, and ways of thinking and feeling of those with whom I had relationships: my fellow workers; the volunteers; the professionals in other areas of service; and, most importantly, the young people who frequented the center and the residents of the neighborhood itself.

True, I did not lack a certain sophistication. I had been reared and educated to be courteous and considerate, and in general I already had positive relationships with others; but I was competitive and not a little haughty. My participation in these sessions taught me some other things, including a sense of responsibility, accountability for my behavior, and a keen self-awareness. I still committed many errors in judgment, and I was frequently confused as to my own motives; but in the main I helped to lead a center bustling with activity, to maintain a semblance of peace in the neighborhood, and to promote cooperative endeavor among the community's young people.

This position would prove to be the unassuming start to a long career as a community organizer. Bringing together many professionals within our community—such as the school principal, social workers, probation and parole officers, health-department nurses, juvenile police officers, and others—we formed the South-of-Seventh-Street Workers, holding brown-bag lunch meetings twice a month to discuss our common concerns, plans, and objectives.

Largely as a result of my work at the center, I was named a Fellow of the John Hay Whitney Foundation, entered the School of Social Welfare at the University of California-Berkeley, and received a Master of Social Welfare degree in Social Group Work in 1953.

For my field-work assignment, I served in Neuro-Psychiatric Service at the Oak Knoll Naval Hospital, working in a locked ward of young sailors and marines. I grew to know the patients, and accompanied them during their routines, even while they waited in fear for the application of electric shock treatment. Some of the consequences of this work were deeply touching. At the end of nine months, the doors and windows of the ward were no longer locked, and the entire ward of patients could travel, as a supervised group, to the recreation center that was a part of the hospital complex.

Upon graduation, I took a position as a social group worker and teacher in the Contra Costa County Juvenile Hall, and then I returned to Oakland's Recreation Department as its community relations consultant. The most tangible manifestation of my work here was in the forming of the Associated Agencies of Oakland, a coalition that brought together seven major government institutions involved with the city's youth and families: the local public schools; Oakland's police department and recreation department; the county's welfare, health, and probation departments; and, from the state level, the California Youth Authority. Such alliances are commonplace now, but some fifty years ago this may well have been one of the first formal partnerships formed among service institutions of government.

The expansion of this program led to my engagement as its coordinator, and I became the first black employed in the city manager's office. Largely as a result of this work and my concurrent political activities, Gov. Edmund G. "Pat" Brown appointed me to the California Commission on Metropolitan Area Problems. I focused my advocacy on increased representation from minority communities and on improved cooperation among the various public entities attempting—and sometimes competing—to be of service to the same populations.

Paul Ylvisaker, a vice-president of the Ford Foundation, attended meetings of the commission. At one point he approached me and asked me, "Evelio, can you attend a meeting in New York next Wednesday?" Thus it was that I became a member of the so-called Great Cities Committee of the Ford Foundation. Its goal was to help the foundation decide how to structure major grants it planned to make to distressed cities across the country. The objective was to help big-city governments to find the right paths to renew their core metropolitan areas.

We visited cities including Pittsburgh, Chicago, New York, Boston, and Washington, D. C.; and we had lively exchanges with school superintendents; city administrators; police chiefs; with directors of city departments such as recreation, welfare, and health; and others.

At a final committee meeting at Ford Foundation headquarters in New York, Paul Ylvisaker once again turned to me. This time he announced to the group: "The most interesting noises I have heard on these trips have come from a city that we did not visit. They came from Oakland, California." He continued, "Evelio, the Ford Foundation would entertain with interest a proposal from the City of Oakland."

In 1961, the Ford Foundation announced its first "Great Cities" grant, for two million dollars, to the City of Oakland for a program of community development. It was submitted as a collaborative proposal by thirteen agencies of the city, Alameda County, the state, the Urban League, and the Community Welfare Council. This was the first grant made to a relatively large consortium of agencies that had agreed to cooperate so as to integrate the various services rendered to the same population. We named the program the Oakland Interagency Council. The grant was renewed for several years and served as a model for federal grants to other cities that followed.

Taking an active role in politics for the first time, I began to use my experience and education in the organization behind Assemblyman William Byron Rumford, the first black elected to office in northern California and only the second elected in the entire state. His field representative, D. G. Gibson, became one of the foremost leaders of the state Democratic Party. He made me his assistant. I could not have wanted a more effective teacher, and a nobler role model.

A grizzled veteran of the long struggle to develop the political power of black Californians, D. G. taught me all that he could in our frequent long discussions. He also taught by example, and I worked by his side for seventeen years. Though offered the opportunity, I never sought political office; I did not believe I had the sort of personality appropriate to the demands of elected office. I was happily established as an organizer and enabler of others. I had the pleasure during these years of playing a part in the development and the rise to power of city-council members, mayors, superior court judges, state supreme court justices, state assemblymen, and a state assemblywoman who later became a member of the United States Congress. Most importantly, I played a major role in projecting the presence the black and Mexican-American electorates.

As "Get Out The Vote" director, I believe I played a significant role in the campaign to elect Judge Lionel Wilson as the first black mayor of Oakland. Later, I would draw own my experience to organize for Mayor Wilson the Oakland Interagency Council on Drugs—a consortium of twenty-three city, county, state, and federal government agencies and community organizations that aimed to prevent drug use and to rehabilitate the drug-addicted.

With respect to Hispanic Americans, I had a major role developing the Community Service Organization, which was created with the guidance of the celebrated Saul Alinsky. I became a part-time paid organizer of the Industrial Areas Foundation, and for one year I served (under Alinsky's tutelage) with Fred Ross, Herman Gallegos, Abelicio Chavez, and Cesar Chavez in the corps of organizers of the Community Service Organization in California. I also gave some support and some guidance to another political organization that sprang from the Community Service Organization, the Mexican-American Political Association (MAPA).

The Spanish-Speaking Unity Council became the most outstanding development flowing from my work with Mexican Americans. Its founder was Arabella Martinez, who received a John Hay Whitney Foundation fellowship upon my nomination. (The council's funding was facilitated by Herman Gallegos, then president of the Southwest Council of La Raza, who also received a John Hay Whitney Fellowship upon my nomination.) Arabella Martinez subsequently became, under President Jimmy Carter, Assistant Secretary for Human Development Services at the Department of Health,

Education, and Welfare (HEW). She took me to Washington to serve as her Executive Assistant for Policy Development.

The Spanish-Speaking Unity Council is today vibrantly alive. It has a long history of social, housing, and economic development programs in the Oakland area. I served as a consultant for many years to the council and to its employment-training subsidiary, the Peralta Service Corporation. For three years I also served as a consultant to the National Hispanic University, then located in Oakland. I helped the board primarily in its attempts to secure state accreditation.

Now in retirement, I am still active in political organizing, though simply as a regular participant in the monthly meetings of my local Democratic club. Throughout the many years, however, when I played a leading role in Oakland politics, I was also active in nonpartisan organizations, serving as vice-president and membership chairman of our local NAACP chapter; as chairman of Oakland Men of Tomorrow, a service organization; as chairman of the Bay Area Black United Fund; and as founder of the Negro Political Action Association of California.

My education and experience have shown me that organizing can manifest itself in service to groups, institutions, political organizations, and communities. I have found myself viewing all these entities as organisms— each one having its own particular history of development: intellectual, emotional, social, and cultural.

Strengthened by a sense of profession, and by my own ideals, I believe that I was useful. I enjoyed, with zest, my opportunities to further the goal of mutual empowerment—empowerment to develop the kind of harmonious world in which we all seek to live.